Go to http://www.FriendshipCenter.com/hearts/ to:

- ♥ Find reading groups at local bookstores.

- ♥ Join online discussion groups.

- ♥ Order recommended books.

- ♥ Sign up for our free mailing list.

Publication Date: May 4, 2003
Advance edition for reviewers — December 19, 2002 (53,730 words)

Published by Thomas David Kehoe
P.O. Box 7551
Boulder, CO 80306-7551

Publisher Cataloging-In-Publication Data
Kehoe, Thomas David
Hearts And Minds: How Our Brains Are Hardwired For Relationships
Includes bibliographical references and index.

ISBN 0-9657181-4-X   SAN 299-2566
Library of Congress Control Number: 2002090500
Library of Congress Subject Heading: HQ801.K45 2003 (Man-woman
    relationships)
Dewey Decimal Classification: 646.77 (Dating and choice of mate)
BASIC: Family & Relationships/Love & Romance
BIC Standard Subject Category: VFHM
ONIX file available from http://www.NetRead.com

Front cover art by Danielle Bustillo
Back cover photo by Rose Simpson
Printed in the United States of America

ACKNOWLEDGEMENTS
Thanks to Eleanor Alden, Gail Hunter, R. Don Steele, Christine
Robertson, Martin Lloyd-Elliot, Anne Marie Wenzel, Alice B.
Kehoe, Darius Baer, Mary Anne Siderits, Rebecca Johnson, Jaak
Panksepp, Phyllis Funari, Paul Goldstein, Steve Nakamoto, Shane
Scaglione, Dan Sturgis, Steven Torrente, Dan Pierce, Lorin Dytell,
Michelle Nagell, and Lara Vracarich.

 Printed with soy ink on recycled paper.

TABLE OF CONTENTS

THE EVOLUTION OF THE HUMAN BRAIN

Large brains are humans' most distinctive anatomical feature. Our brains are about four times bigger than chimpanzees' and gorillas' brains.

Brains use twenty times the calories of muscles at rest. Brains require maintaining a constant temperature. Large brains are easily injured, and make childbirth difficult. Intelligence has many costs, yet doesn't directly help an animal survive (e.g., a big brain doesn't make you run faster or survive colder weather).

Our ancestors' brains began to enlarge about two million years ago. In evolutionary time, two million years is short. Why our ancestors rapidly evolved large brains—specifically, a large, uniquely human *cerebral cortex*—is the central question of human evolution.

The Triune Brain

Our brains comprise three distinct structures, representing three evolutionary periods.[1]

The oldest, deepest, and smallest area is the *reptilian brain*.[2] The reptilian brain controls the heart, lungs, and other vital organs. It enables aggression, mating, and reaction to immediate danger.

Mammals evolved the *limbic system*. This is the middle layer of our brains, surrounding the reptilian brain. The physiological features unique to mammals are in the limbic brain, e.g., the hypothalamus system for keeping us warm.

The limbic brain also produces emotions. Emotions facilitate relationships. Mammals, unlike reptiles, care for their young. Mammals evolved brains hardwired for mother-child and other relationships.

> The most common reaction a reptile has to its young is indifference; it lays its eggs and walks (or slithers) away. Mammals form close-knit, mutually nurturant social groups—families—in which members spend time touching and caring for one another. Parents nourish and safeguard their young, and each other, from the hostile world outside their group. A mammal will risk and sometimes lose its life to protect a child or mate from attack. A garter snake or salamander watches the death of its kin with an unblinking eye.[3]
> — Thomas Lewis, Fari Amini, and Richard Lannon
> *A General Theory of Love* (2000)

The *cerebral cortex* (or *neocortex*) is the newest, outermost area of our brains. The oldest mammals, e.g., opossums, have only a thin layer of cerebral cortex. Rabbits have a little more, cats a bit more. Monkeys have a substantial cerebral cortex. Humans—and only humans—have an enormous cerebral cortex.[4]

The cerebral cortex learns new things. Animals with little or no cerebral cortex act only as their genes program them to act. Animals with a cerebral cortex can find new foods, survive in new environments, or change their mating tactics to improve reproductive success.

The human cerebral cortex goes beyond learning new foods and survival skills. Our brains can think in abstractions. We communicate via symbols (e.g., language), consider the past and future, and sacrifice our personal interests not only for our families (as other mammals do) but also for ideas (e.g., honor and country).

Conflicts between brain areas lead to relationship difficulties. In a conflicted brain, the older area wins. In contrast, an individual with an *integrated* brain—i.e., who uses his or her whole brain—solves relationship problems.

Ontogeny Recapitulates Phylogeny

A child's development mimics its species' evolution.

Infants live in their reptilian brains. They eat, breathe, crawl, sleep, etc.

Children live in their limbic brains. They feel emotions strongly. They use emotions to form relationships.

Adolescents live in their cerebral cortexes. They strive to become unique individuals. They quest to find abstract principles to live by.

Adult relationships invert childhood development. Men and women use cerebral cortex abstractions (e.g., gender roles) to attract opposite sex partners. If a couple then feels limbic brain emotionally connected "chemistry," they form a relationship. If the relationship goes well, sooner or later they're in bed, using their reptilian brains.

Love develops a child's limbic brain.[5] Unloved children fail to develop limbic brains capable of emotional intimacy. Such an individual can relate on a reptilian level—e.g., food, warmth, sex— or on a cerebral cortex level—e.g., excelling at accounting or the law —but have difficulty with intimacy.

Natural vs. Sexual Selection

In *The Origin of Species* (1859), Charles Darwin wrote that species evolve via random mutations. Environmental changes—e.g., changing food sources, predation, climate—favor one mutation over another. He called this process *natural selection*.

The conventional view is that our smarter, larger-brained ancestors invented tools, and then dominated their smaller-brained relations. The archaeological facts don't support this "man the toolmaker" hypothesis.

Our ancestors first used stone tools 2.5 million years, or 100,000 generations, ago.[6] This book has about 50,000 words. To refer to the first human as your "great-great-great...grandparent," you'd have to replace every word in this book with "great," and you'd need two books.

After one million years, or near the end of the first book, our ancestors' brains were more than double in size. Archaeologists can see slight improvements in their stone tools.[7]

500,000 years ago—halfway through the second book—our ancestors' brains were nearly as big as our brains. Our ancestors started using fire.[8] Fire enabled them to move from Africa to colder Europe and Asia.

50,000 years ago—eight pages from the end of the second book —our ancestors' brains reached modern size. Their stone tools became thinner and sharper. They carved small ornamental figurines from ivory, shell, and stone. They created beautiful cave paintings. They built the first ocean-going boats.[9]

5,000–10,000 years ago—the last page of the second book—our ancestors developed agriculture. Poor nutrition made farmers' bodies and brains smaller. They invented writing and metal tools. They invented the bow and arrow—a weapon that seems primitive to us.[10]

Our ancestors' brains enlarged *before* technological advances. Our ancestors' brains were ready for modern technology long before they invented it. Tool use was a *spandrel* or side effect of large brains. Something else drove human brain evolution.

Sexual Selection

In *The Descent of Man* (1871), Darwin wrote that natural selection failed to explain human evolution. Instead, he proposed an alternative theory. Species evolve when males and females select each other for certain qualities. He called this *sexual selection*. Biologists ignored this idea for over a century.[11]

Females are more selective than males. Females do most of the work of producing and raising children. In contrast, fathering a child is less work, so males aren't so choosy.

> The exertion of some choice on the part of the female seems almost as general a law as the eagerness of the male.[12]
> — Charles Darwin, *The Descent of Man* (1871)

Females choose males with features that make the males *less* able to survive.[13] E.g., a peacock's bright colors make him visible to predators, and his huge tail slows his escapes. His beautiful tail communicates to peahens that he's an especially fit individual, i.e., he's so fast that he can escape predators despite his heavy tail. Sexual selection is, in general, the opposite of natural selection.

Natural selection advances via slow environmental change. Natural selection advances evolution only in harsh environments (e.g., predation, climate change). Natural selection produces animals better able to survive—usually smaller, more efficient, and less conspicuous.

In contrast, sexual selection advances with each generation. Sexual selection produces rapid evolutionary changes. Sexual selection advances evolution in stable environments. Sexual selection produces animals (especially males) less able to survive, with bigger, brighter, or exaggerated features.

What's Sexy About a Cerebral Cortex?

Humans' oversized brains could have evolved due to sexual selection. But what's sexy about an enlarged cerebral cortex? Women don't say, "Look at the cerebral cortex on that dude! I want to have his children!" Our ancestors must have instead been attracted to cerebral cortex *behaviors*.

Our cerebral cortexes enable many behaviors, e.g., speech and language. But what's striking about the cerebral cortex is how much of it is *not* dedicated to specific behaviors. The human cerebral cortex has billions of general-purpose neurons, capable of learning any new idea. Why were our ancestral mothers and fathers—unlike any other animals—sexually attracted to partners who could learn new ideas?

Monogamy and Lying

Most mammal fathers have little or no involvement with their offspring.[14] Male gorillas kill infants fathered by other males. Male chimpanzees help all the youngsters in their group, but they don't know who fathered each child.

Human evolution may have begun when fathers helped raise their children, giving their children a survival advantage. Among hunter-gatherers today, children without fathers are more than twice as likely to die during childhood.[15]

Monogamy caused a conflict between two reproductive strategies. A man could try to have sex with many women, risking rejection from women, violence from other men, or his fatherless children not surviving. Such a man might father no surviving children.

Or a man could choose a monogamous relationship. Such a man would father only a few children, but his children would survive and prosper.

A woman could have sex with a desirable (e.g., high-status, tall, strong, handsome) man, and risk competing women taking him from her. Or she could choose a stable, monogamous relationship with a less-desirable man whom no one other woman wanted.

Both men and women could have increased reproductive success by lying. The most basic lie is for a woman to get pregnant by a physically desirable (but uncommitted) man, and then tell her committed (but less desirable) partner that the child is his.

Or a woman can lie to a less-desirable man that she'll marry him (i.e., keep him as an insurance policy), while dating more desirable men in hope that one will marry her.

Or a woman can lie to a desirable man, who's committed to another woman, that she only wants a short-term sexual relationship. She then leaves an earring in his bed for his wife to find. If she can break up his marriage, he might marry her.

Men's basic lie is to promise commitment to women, have sex, and then leave. Or a man committed to one woman could secretly commit to a second woman, perhaps in a neighboring village.

Sexual Lying Could Have Driven Cerebral Cortex Development
Getting caught reduces a liar's reproductive success. Catching liars increases the lie-catcher's reproductive success.

Lying requires imagination, quick thinking, and, above all,

thinking of new lies. Catching lies requires imagination, quick thinking, and a long memory.

Those are cerebral cortex activities. Effective liars also match their emotions to their lies. You catch lies when an individual's emotional state doesn't match his or her words. Effective lying requires integrating one's cerebral cortex with one's limbic brain.

A man or woman with a larger cerebral cortex, well-integrated with his or her limbic brain, is better able to sexually lie, and to catch sexual lies. Such men and women became our ancestors.

HOW WOMEN SELECT MEN

Women have two, conflicting instincts when choosing men. On the one hand, women want superior men, a.k.a. "alpha" males. On the other hand, women want men who can materially provide for their families, commit to a long-term relationship, and enjoy interacting with children, a.k.a. "good relationship skills."

"Alpha" Males

What kind of "alpha" male are you?

If you're a gorilla, you're big and strong. You're twice the size of a female. You fight any male you meet. You live with your harem of two to five females. Your females are monogamously faithful to you. Your penis is one inch long. Sex is quick.

If you're a gibbon, you mate monogamously for life. You live with your mate and your children. You sing to your mate. She sings back to let you know where she is. You and your mate are the same size and look identical. You start each morning with a half-hour of loud hooting to frighten other gibbons away from your forty acres of forest.

If you're a chimpanzee, you live in a group of fifty individuals. When a female is ovulating, she has sex with every male in the group. You have a large penis, large testicles, and ejaculate lots of sperm. You reproduce not because you dominate females or other males, but because your sperm is more active than other males' sperm.

If you're a baboon, you live in a troop that varies from 10 to 200 individuals, depending on habitat, time of year, and predation.[16] You make friends with other males. When another male threatens you, your friends back you up. You avoid fighting. Fighting leads to injuries, and lions eat injured baboons.[17] You also make friends with females. Female baboons mate with their male friends. They like males who have many friends.

Women Go For Tail Feathers

Among the Aché hunter-gatherers of Paraguay, the men hunt big-game animals. They bring home a big animal about one day in ten. They return empty-handed the other days. Men, on median, bring in 4,663 calories per day.

Aché women gather plants and small animals, and care for their children (see "How Our Ancestors Lived," page 29). The amount of food a woman brings home depends only on how many hours she spends laboriously picking and processing foods. Women, on average, bring in 10,356 calories per day.

When an Aché man brings home a deer, he shares it with other families, not only with his wife and children. Why do Aché men hunt large animals, only to give away this relatively rare food? Why not help their wives gather food? Such a man could easily bring home enough plants and small animals for two wives and their children.

Aché women view big-game hunting like peahens view peacocks' tail feathers. Big-game hunting shows that a man is physically and mentally fit. Giving away meat shows that he has more than enough strength and skill to survive. Women like men with many friends, and giving away meat maintains friendships. Men give meat to lower-status individuals to show their superior place in the social hierarchy (see "The Great Male Hierarchy," page 61).

Extramarital sex isn't unusual among the Aché. When asked who had fathered their children, Aché women named, on average, 2.1 possible fathers for each child. On the list of possible fathers, the best hunters' names came up most often.

Status

Women prefer high-status men.[18] In workplace affairs, men are equally likely to have sex with a superior or subordinate woman. Women, in contrast, are seven times more likely to have sex with superior, rather than subordinate, men.[19]

Many societies expect the sons of leaders to become leaders. Women who want "alpha" sons marry "alpha" husbands. E.g., the 2000 presidential election was between the son of a president, the son of a senator, the son and grandson of four-star Navy admirals, and the son of a wealthy banker (George W. Bush, Al Gore, John McCain, and Bill Bradley).

To attract women, improve your social status. Give away stuff to make friends. Help less-fortunate individuals, to show that you're above average. Lead groups, e.g., captain your softball team. Dress well. Speak well, perhaps by joining Toastmasters International (http://www.toastmasters.org/).

Money

Women are conflicted about money. Women want "alpha" males who show off their money like peacocks show off their tail feathers, e.g., buying a round of drinks in a bar. But women also want "relationship" men who put their paychecks into a mortgage.

Show off your money to attract a woman's attention. Then talk about the home you're buying to make her want a relationship.

Our hunter-gatherer ancestors owned nothing but what they could carry to the next campsite. Accumulation of wealth wasn't possible. Women's cerebral cortexes have learned to appreciate accumulated wealth, but their brains aren't hardwired for this. In a conflict, women choose their older instinct—love—instead of their newer appreciation of wealth.

Confidence and Stress

Aché men gamble on bringing home a deer one day in ten, instead of choosing the safety of helping their wives gather food. Gambling—and a man's life in general—is stressful.

Mammals produce glucocorticoid hormones in stressful situations. Too much glucocorticoid causes health problems. In male and female primates, high-status individuals produce minimal glucocorticoid in stressful situations. Low-status individuals produce too much glucocorticoid.[20] Stress—"the fear of fear itself"—physically hurts low-status individuals. Stress doesn't affect the health of high-status individuals.

Confident men—who believe that their powers or circumstances can handle stressful situations—attract women.[21] To attract women *and* improve your health, take a stress-reduction class. Learn to handle stressful situations with confidence.

The common belief that men are hardwired to be alone ("go to their caves") after a stressful day and that women are hardwired to talk to a supportive partner is a misconception. The former is the *avoidant attachment style* and the latter is the *secure attachment style*. It's true that attachment styles are hardwired in adults, and it's true that this distinction is of paramount importance in relationships (mismatched partners have more relationship difficulties, and avoidant individuals have more relationship difficulties in general) but the hardwiring is from the individual's early childhood relationship with his or her mother. Men and women can have either attachment style.

Looks, Height, and Strength

Women rate tall, strong, athletic males as "very desirable" marriage partners. Women value physical strength in men about twice as highly as men value physical strength in women.

However, women prefer men with feminine-looking faces. E.g., women prefer Leonardo DiCaprio to Tom Selleck.[22]

American women prefer men 5'11" (1.8 meters) or taller.[23] Tall men receive more personal ad responses than short men.

If you're short, study Japanese. Then vacation on Guam, the Hawaii-like American island where Japanese women vacation.

Never-married women are more likely to prefer physical attractiveness. Conversely, divorced and widowed women are more likely to select good character over physical attractiveness.

Age

Women select personal ads primarily by age.[24] Women select men who are, on average, three and a half years older. Older men, in general, have more social status and emotional maturity.

The worldwide average age difference between brides and

grooms is three years. Americans marry closer in age.[25]

In 1890, the average age at which men first married was 26. Women married at 22 (see Figure 1: Age At First Marriage).[26]

During the first half of the twentieth century, increasing affluence enabled younger men to support families. Secondary education and increased leisure time facilitated dating. Dating sometimes led to sex, pregnancy, and early marriage. In 1956, men married at 22, women at 20.

The FDA approved oral contraceptives in 1956. The Supreme Court legalized abortion in 1973. Women delayed motherhood to start careers.[27] In 1998, men married at 27, women at 25.

Couples now live together from the age that their parents' generation married. The average man now first lives with a woman, either in marriage or as an unmarried couple, for the first time at 22. The average woman moves in with a man at age 20 or 21.[28]

Couples that marry younger than 25 have dramatically higher divorce rates.[29]

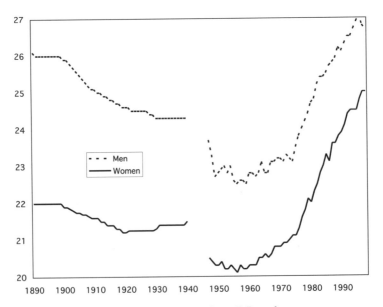

Figure 1: Age At First Marriage

Relationship Skills

Women want men who'll stay in a faithful, long-term relationship. But a woman can't predict a man's behavior twenty years in the future. Women instead look for signs that a man is relationship material.

Predictability

Women prefer men who have a steady job, are dependable, and are emotionally stable.[30] A predictable man may be boring, but a woman feels that she can predict his behavior twenty years into the future. Unpredictable, "flighty" men turn off women.

E.g., if you want to date a certain waitress, eat at her restaurant every day for months, at the same time each day, ask for the same table, and order the same meal (and leave the same big tip).

Home Ownership

One of the highest factors correlating with likelihood of a man to marry is home ownership.[31]

If you own a home, when asking a woman out, give her your business card and write your home address on the back. She'll drive by and look at your home. On a date, talk about your home.

If you don't own a home, say that you've been looking at homes to buy. Women enjoy talking about buying homes.

Family Relationships

Another sign that a man will be a good husband and father is his relationship with his family. Show women photos of yourself playing with your nieces and nephews. Invite your date to meet your siblings or cousins and their nieces and nephews (meeting your parents and grandparents is less effective).

Men positively interacting with children attract women. Men who ignore a child in distress turn off women. Women's favorite pinups show bare-chested, muscled men holding smiling babies.

In contrast, men have no preference for women interacting with children versus women alone.[32] E.g., men like pinups of bare-chested women, but not holding babies.

Astrology and Personality Types

Astrology and personality types fascinate women. They hope to predict the future of their relationships. Talk about personality types on dates (see "Archetypes," page 153).

Or put astrology software on your laptop computer. If a party is boring, sit down at the kitchen table and offer to do astrology charts.

Emotional Connection

The prefrontal lobes (part of the cerebral cortex) enable *affect-regulation*, or the

> ability to regulate our emotional reactions, control our impulses, or moderate the survival reflexes of our ancient reptilian system.[33]
> — Joseph Chilton Pearce, *The Biology of Transcendence* (2002)

The prefrontal lobes are our most recently evolved brain area.[34] This is also the last area to develop in each individual—maturing between the ages of 15 and 21.[35]

Women want emotionally mature men. An emotionally mature man changes his emotions as situations change—or to change a situation. Although his limbic brain experiences a wide range of emotions, his higher self (his prefrontal lobes) stays constant. Such an individual is capable of a long-term relationship.

E.g., in *Roxanne* (1987), a man insults Steve Martin. Martin at first shows anger at the insult. But then he switches to humor. Martin first makes jokes about himself. Then he switches the subject of his wit to the other man, making a crowd laugh at the man. The other man shows only one emotion—anger—in response to each of Martin's emotions.

Imagine that your emotions are like a car with a standard transmission. To shift from one emotion to another, you shift through neutral. In neutral, you quiet one emotion before shifting to another emotion. When you quiet your own emotions, you can feel your partner's emotions. Buddhists call this state *egoless*. Christians say *selfless*. When you feel your partner's emotions, you can select the best emotion for the situation.

Fear Reduces Us to Reptilian Responses

You meet an attractive woman. Your cerebral cortex imagines your friends' envy if she goes out with you.

Your limbic brain fears that she'll reject you.

Your reptilian brain wants to have sex with her.

In a conflicted brain, the older brain area wins. You're capable of having sex with her. Your reptilian brain is perfectly functional.

Your limbic brain is warning, "Don't emotionally connect with her! You'll get hurt!" You're unable to feel her emotional state. She seems like a beautiful statue in a museum.

You've locked out your cerebral cortex. Language is a cerebral cortex activity, so you can only stare at her breasts and mumble incoherently.

> When integrated, [the triune brain] offers us an open-ended potential; an ability to rise and go beyond all constraint or limitation. But when that integration fails, our mind is a house divided against itself, our behavior a paradoxical civil war—and we become our own worst enemy.[36]
> — Joseph Chilton Pearce, *The Biology of Transcendence* (2002)

Developing Awareness of Choices

Cerebral cortex activity won't get you out of an internal conflict. E.g., repeating positive statements (*affirmations*) while blocking awareness of your emotional state won't help.

Instead, connect to your limbic brain. Feel your emotional state.

Slow down. When you react quickly, your brain selects *myelinated* or habitual responses. Instead of going with your first reaction, pause and breathe.

Imagine your choices. Imagine alternative responses.

No one needs to be completely hemmed in by circum-

stances; no one needs to be the victim of his biography.[37]
— George Kelly, *The Psychology of Personal Constructs*
(1955)

Think through your general fear to specific fears. E.g., you fear that she'll say that you're too old for her. Imagine different responses you could make to that rejection:

> When Hugh Hefner first asked Barbi Benton out, she said, "Well, I've, uh, never dated anyone over 23 before."
> Hef responded without hesitation, "That's okay. Neither have I."[38]

You'll no longer feel fear. What seemed like an insurmountable problem now looks like a variety of choices, each leading to a positive conclusion.

Imagining different possible futures is a cerebral cortex activity. Feeling emotions is a limbic brain activity. Imagining your emotions in various scenarios connects your cerebral cortex and limbic brain. You unblock your internal conflicts.

Play a Game

When an unexpected event upsets you, the problem isn't the event. The problem is that you don't know how to respond. When you're upset you fail to see positive opportunities. You see only that your plans are blocked. Instead, stay flexible and look for opportunities in unexpected events.

E.g., a man sees a woman sitting in a bar booth. He walks over, bends down to talk to her, and bonks his head on a lampshade hanging over the table. Momentarily stunned, he stands there while the lampshade swings back and bonks his head a second time.

He says, "Excuse me. Let me do this again." He returns to his bar stool. He comes back to the woman, puts his hand calmly on the lampshade, bends down, and introduces himself.

This happened to one of my friends. He and the woman dated for several months.

He managed his fear by playing a game. Play boosts emotional experience, and develops relationships with other individuals.

Children play obvious games. Adults play subtle games. Let's make my friend's game more obvious:

Shift to a pretend world. He said, in effect, "I'm going to *pretend* to meet you." In pretend worlds we're less afraid of showing emotions.

Focus on a bipolar construct. Psychologists call a pair of opposite ideas a *bipolar construct.* A literature major would say *irony.* Whatever you call it, when an individual does two, opposite things at the same time, we laugh. In this game, the bipolar construct was being cool vs. being clumsy.

Exaggerate emotions. If my friend had played the game to entertain a child, he would've amplified his emotions. E.g., he returns to his bar stool. Then he pretends to see the woman for the first time. His eyes pop open and his jaw drops. His hand shakes and he nearly spills his beer in his lap. He exaggerates preening in the bar mirror, then swaggers over.

Repeat the game. If he were playing the game to entertain a child, he'd bonk his head on the lampshade—three times. Then he'd repeat the skit. He could repeat it thirty times and the child would laugh every time.

Exchange roles. If he were entertaining a child, he'd trade places with the child. The child would pretend to be clumsy Joe Cool.

Make your game physical and unstructured. Children play physical, unstructured, non-competitive games. Adults play abstract, non-physical, structured, competitive games, e.g., spectator sports, casino gambling, ballroom dancing, and board games. My friend's game was physical (bonking his head on the lampshade) and unstructured (he didn't hand out a sheet of rules).

Schedule playtime. For your next party, tell your guests that the first hour will be games, e.g., Twister. Find free, fun party games at http://www.FriendshipCenter.com/hearts/.

Laugh to Connect Your Limbic Brain and Cerebral Cortex

Only humans laugh. Other animals express emotions as they occur. Our emotional regulation stops us from suddenly expressing unexpected emotions.

Our cerebral cortex sends emotions it doesn't know how to regulate to our speech area, and we laugh. We associate laughter with humor because humor is always unexpected. But humor isn't one emotion. Humor is any emotion we can't regulate. Because different individuals regulate different emotions well or poorly, different individuals laugh at different events.

A sense of humor attracts women. Laugh in emotional situations, e.g., when you do something embarrassing. Laughing connects your limbic brain and cerebral cortex, enabling better awareness of your emotions.

Reveal a Secret to Emotionally Connect

In 1957, a young man arrived in Nashville. He stuttered, but played guitar, and could sing without stuttering.

Soon he had a job performing with Minnie Pearl, the country comedienne. Pearl encouraged him to talk on stage. He refused, afraid that the audience would laugh at his speech.

Pearl replied:

> Let 'em laugh. Goodness gracious, laughs are hard to get and I'm sure that they're laughing with you and not against you, Melvin.[39]

The singer developed humorous routines about his stuttering. Audiences laughed. His career took off.

> Word began to circulate around Nashville about this young singer from Florida who could write songs and sing, but stuttered like hell when he tried to talk. The next thing I knew I was being asked to be on every major television show in America.[40]
>
> — Mel Tillis

Don't be afraid to share a secret. Women share secrets with girlfriends to emotionally connect (see "Women's Support Circles," page 62). But don't whine about your problems. Instead, talk confidently about a secret to show that you've turned a weakness into strength.

Entertainment Skills

Entertainment expresses emotions. Effective entertainers emotionally connect with their audiences.

Entertainment integrates limbic brain emotions with cerebral cortex imagination. When an entertainer expresses an old emotion in a new way, we applaud.

Other animals do the same mating rituals generation after generation. E.g., peahens never get bored watching peacocks show off their tail feathers. Like peahens, older women enjoy 300-year-old operas. But young women want only new music, the latest clothes, and the coolest actors. Their greatest put-down is "that's so ten minutes ago."

> Mankind might well be a tool-making and tool-using species, but nothing so separates us from the lower animals than our almost comic enthusiasm for the new, new thing.[41]
> — Nick Schultz, editor of TechCentralStation.com

Effective entertainers have integrated brains. Conversely, to improve your brain integration, develop your entertainment skills.

Entertaining men attract women. When a man's performance makes a woman feel emotionally connected, her limbic brain tells her that she's in a long-term relationship with him.

A woman with an integrated brain responds, "I want a long-term relationship with this man. I'll buy his CDs (or watch his movies). I'll feel as if I've known him for years."

A woman with a poorly integrated brain might try to have a physical relationship with the man, even though her cerebral cortex tells her that he'll never commit to a relationship with her. In a conflicted brain, the older area wins.

Entertainment skills can make women ignore a man's faults. E.g., Woody Allen's sense of humor attracts women, even though he's small, scrawny, and his idea of a relationship is marrying his stepdaughter.[42] (At least he's a family man.)

Women's Entertainment Skills

Male entertainers, in general, have both male and female fans. Female entertainers, until recently, had only female fans, and had fewer fans than male entertainers. E.g., your local ballet company has fewer fans than your professional basketball team.

Masculine individuals (generally, but not always, men) use entertainment skills to attract sexual partners. Feminine individuals (generally, but not always, women) use entertainment skills to keep a partner in a long-term relationship.

E.g., a woman who makes her husband laugh each day, and makes his heart ache when she sings lullabies to their children, has a husband who's not going to leave her.

Legendary King Shahryar took a new woman to bed each night, and then killed each woman in the morning. One woman saved herself by telling a story with a cliffhanger ending. Shahrazad kept this up night after night, spinning Ali Baba and the Forty Thieves, Sinbad the Sailor, and other stories into *One Thousand and One Arabian Nights* (circa A.D. 1000).

Truth and Lying in Art and Entertainment

Entertainment skills increase reproductive success so effectively (i.e., get women to have sex with men, and get men to stay with women) that sexual selection for entertainment skills may have driven our ancestors to evolve larger cerebral cortexes.[43]

Art and entertainment are lies, from the point of view of the liar. E.g., when an actor playing Hamlet says that he's going to kill his stepfather, the actor isn't threatening his stepfather's life. A painter creates an image that looks real, but isn't. A poem makes us visualize a scene we don't see. Novels and movies take us into a worlds we've never experienced.

But art and entertainment are truthful, from the point of view of the audience. Effective artists and entertainers communicate emotions that "strike a chord" in the listener or viewer. They tell the truth not about themselves—e.g., you don't want to know that an actor is afraid of forgetting his lines, or is hoping that a movie producer might be in the audience and offer him a better-paying job —but instead quiet their own emotions and instead emote the audience's feelings.

Religion and Evolution

Religious art, music, and storytelling move our emotions more than any other form of entertainment.

Art, entertainment, religion, and reproductive success are entwined. Religious men and women sing in church or synagogue, dramatically recite Bible stories, dance at rituals, etc.

Most societies encourage religious men, e.g., rabbis, to marry and produce large families. Men prefer to marry religious women, because they're more likely to be sexually faithful.

Our ancestors' sexual preference for partners with deeply moving emotional skills may have driven them to evolve brains capable of spiritual thought. I.e., evolution enabled humans to think spirituality, and, conversely, spiritual thinking may have driven human evolution.

Consumerism as Runaway Sexual Selection

For our ancestral fathers, entertainment was "do it yourself." Dinner was killing and roasting an animal. After dinner, they played music, danced, or told epics of their heroes.

Now consider what happens in modern courtship. We take our dates to restaurants where we pay professional chefs to cook them great food, or to dance clubs where professional musicians excite their auditory systems, or to films where professional actors entertain them with vicarious adventures. The chefs, musicians, and actors do not actually have sex with our dates. They just get paid. We get the sex if the date goes well. Of course, we still have to talk in modern courtship, and we still have to look reasonably good. But the market economy shifts much of the courtship effort from us to professionals. To pay the professionals, we have to make money, which means getting a job. The better our education, the better our job,

the more money we make, and the better the vicarious courtship we can afford. Consumerism turns the tables on ancestral patterns of human courtship.[44]
— Geoffrey Miller, *The Mating Mind* (2000)

I can't stand dinner and a movie.[45]
— Julia Schultz, *Playboy* centerfold

Onstage, I make love to 25,000 people—then I go home alone.[46]
— Janis Joplin

Consumerism hotwires our brains' relationship circuits. Cars, shopping malls, television, and Julia Schultz's *Playboy* poses hit these neural circuits.

Women are especially susceptible to consumerism. E.g., on eBay, women described 11% of their shoes as "sexy." Men described only 0.005% of their shoes as "sexy."

Consumerism makes us work longer hours to buy more stuff for our mates. Women have less time to exercise and look attractive. Men have less time to practice entertainment skills. Couples have less time together.

The effects of consumerism range from environmental destruction to anti-American hatred. Runaway consumerism—not war, crime, or disease—is the greatest threat to human survival. Focus on relationships, not buying stuff. You'll be happier and your grandchildren will have a planet to live on.

HOW MEN SELECT WOMEN

You have the most marvelous youth, and youth is the one thing worth having....Someday when you are old and wrinkled and ugly, when thought has seared your forehead with its lines and passion branded your lips with its hideous fires, you will feel it. You will feel it terribly. Now, wherever you go you charm the world. Will it always be so? You have a wonderfully beautiful face, Mr. Gray.... And beauty is a form of genius—is higher, indeed, than genius, as it needs no explanation. It is one of the great facts of the world, like sunlight or springtime or the reflection in dark waters of that silver shell we call the Moon. It cannot be questioned. It has its divine right of sovereignty. It makes princes of those who have it. You smile—ah, when you have lost it you won't smile. People say sometimes that beauty is only superficial. That may be so, but at least it is not so superficial as thought is. To me, beauty is the wonder of wonders. It is only shallow people who do not judge by appearances. The true mystery of the world is the visible, not the invisible.
— Oscar Wilde, *The Picture of Dorian Gray* (1890)

Youth

Women with *high reproductive value* attract men. 19-year-old women are likely to produce the greatest number of children—twice as many as 30-year-old women.

Teenage boys prefer girls a year older. Men in their early twenties prefer women a year or two younger. Thirtysomething men prefer women 5 to 10 years younger. Men in their 40s and 50s prefer women 10 to 20 years younger.

Women of all ages prefer a man a few years older.[47]

Neoteny

Neoteny is the retention of juvenile characteristics into adulthood.

In other primates, e.g., chimpanzees and gorillas, both male and female adults have tough skin, coarse body hair, Adam's apples, and deep voices.

But adult women look and sound like children.[48] Men and women agree that attractive women have the large eyes and lips and small noses and chins of children. Attractive women's faces have the proportions of 11-to-14-year-old children.[49]

Women further neoteny by using cosmetics, shaving their legs, and wearing children's clothing, e.g., Mary Jane shoes.

But men feeling attraction to pre-pubescent girls has no evolutionary value. Women evolved features that distinguish them from girls, yet look nothing like men. These secondary sexual characteristics include prominent breasts, small waists, and full hips.

Children's long dependency on their fathers led to neoteny. Fatherless children—a million years ago or today—were less likely to learn adult skills, inherit social status, and reproduce. Women who looked young were able to keep a man for twenty years, instead of losing him to a younger woman. A young-looking widow could find a second husband.[50] Children with young-looking mothers were more likely to have fathers, and grow up to become our ancestors.

Beauty

Beauty standards are universal across cultures. People around the world have 91–94% agreement about the facial attractiveness of Asian, Hispanic, black, and white women. Even native people unexposed to mass media agree with the rest of the world.

Infants gaze longer and show more pleasure when looking at pictures of attractive male and female faces. One-year-olds play longer with facially attractive dolls than with unattractive dolls.[51]

Beauty standards are cues to a woman's health: clear, smooth skin; full, lustrous hair; full lips; bright eyes; and symmetrical features.

Composite faces, made by combining many photographs on a computer, are more attractive than any individual face. Beauty is "average" looks, not unusual or "striking" features.

Men, in general, don't judge women as being fat or thin. Rather, men consider women with a 70% waist-to-hip ratio to be beautiful. E.g., a woman with a 21-inch waist and 30-inch hips, a woman with a 24-inch waist and 35-inch hips, and a woman with a 28-inch waist and 40-inch hips are equally attractive.[52] The 70% waist-to-hip ratio indicates health and fertility.

Cultural Beauty Standards

Some beauty preferences vary between cultures, e.g., light or dark skin.

When a society experiences rapid change, it values youth and new, iconoclastic ideas. The 1920s and 1960s preferred thin, flat-chested, youthful women.

Conservative societies—e.g., the Victorian era, or the 1950s—value old ideas, and full-figured, fertile adult women. New York and San Francisco value thin women; in contrast, small, rural towns prefer full-figured women.

American women chose thinner-than-average women as the most beautiful. American men prefer average-size women. Fashion models are thinner than porn stars.[53]

Use cultural beauty standards to your advantage. Unlike your ancestors, you can move to a different city or even country. Select a culture where you're beautiful.

Media Effects on Beauty Standards

Our grandparents saw relatively few people. They saw even fewer beautiful people. In contrast, today we turn on a television and see nothing but attractive people made up to look their best, with the bad shots discarded. (Finally, a reason to praise Fox's "reality" television shows!)

Since the 1930s—the beginning of mass advertising and fashion magazines—men have increased the importance of "good looks" in a wife by 40%. Women have increased the importance of a good-looking husband almost 80%. Women in 1996 valued "good looks" in husbands more than men in 1939 valued "good looks" in wives.[54]

Photos of beautiful women made men rate their wives as less attractive, and feel less committed to their marriages, compared to men who looked at photos of "average" women.[55]

Learn the game, then bend the rules. Before submitting a personal ad, have a "makeover" photo studio make you look like a glamorous model. When you marry, get rid of your television.

The media also affect men. Performers such as Jerry Seinfeld raise expectations of men's entertainment skills. As media images make women feel inadequately attractive, media entertainers make men feel inadequately entertaining. These men give up and say that they can't dance, sing, or tell jokes. The positive side is less competition for men who try to entertain women. Older men have an advantage here over younger men. Many young women have never had a man make them laugh, lead them on the dance floor, or play Chopin for an audience of one.

Beautiful Young Women Don't Have It Easy

For beautiful young women, the problem is sorting the wheat from the chaff. Finding a quality mate is no easier for them than for anyone else. They spend as much effort rejecting the wrong men as the rest of us spend getting dates.

In the animal world, females initiate 80% of matings (see "Flirting," page 97). Males who initiate mating are the males that no female will approach. Men who approach women pick young, beautiful women. Q.E.D., beautiful young women meet more than their share of losers.

Dating advice books tell men to ignore a woman to attract her attention. It's not that women like to be ignored. Rather, women know that if a man pays too much attention to a woman, he's a loser. (The converse isn't true—men are attracted to women who pay attention to them.)

If women are too attractive, men stay in their cerebral cortexes. They'll date beautiful women to feel envy from their male friends. They have no reason to shift into their limbic brains and emotionally connect. When men are jerks and women are shallow, they're stuck in their cerebral cortexes.

Putting effort into clothes and make-up will get you more dates, but impair men's vision of your inner beauty. The ideal is to look nice, but don't overdo it. If you're getting many dates but aren't meeting quality men, work on improving yourself, not your wardrobe.

Encourage self-selection of potential mates. Tell suitors that you can't go out on a date, but they're welcome to join you volunteering, e.g., with Habitat For Humanity. The few men who show up to work are the ones worth dating.

Education and Employment

Education, employment, and relationships are problematic for women. On the one hand, school and work are the most common places where couples meet (see "Where Couples Met," page 88). Women who go to college and choose a professional career are more likely to meet men (especially if they choose traditionally male fields, e.g., science). And men prefer to marry women with good educations and good jobs.[56]

On the other hand, career women sometimes must sacrifice relationships. E.g., a job may require moving to a new city. Women who choose professional careers postpone marriage until they're out of college and have started their careers—by which time they find that many of their male classmates and co-workers are married.

Conversely, women whose primary goal is to be a mother are least likely to meet men. Such women forego higher education and professional careers. E.g., a woman who loves children may seek employment in childcare—where she works with other women.

Emotional Connection

Emotional connection makes women want sex. Emotional connection makes men want long-term relationships.

Emotional connection makes men and women switch gender roles (see "Becoming a Couple," page 139). Individuals who use masculine sexuality (usually, but not always, men) want to have sex with many partners. Individuals who use feminine sexuality (usually, but not always, women) want long-term committed relationships. Emotional connection makes women switch to masculine sexuality, and makes men switch to feminine sexuality.

A man using masculine sexuality shows off his social status, physique, and money to attract women's attention. But that's all stereotyped gender roles can do (attract attention). Once he has a woman's attention, she'll look for relationship skills, entertainment skills (e.g., a sense of humor), and, above all, the emotional connection of "chemistry."

A woman using feminine sexuality shows off her youth and beauty to attract men's attention. But that's all her stereotyped gender role can do. If they don't emotionally connect, he'll date her only as long as he thinks he might get to have sex.

Be Seen in Different Venues
Make your suitor feel emotionally connected by letting him see you in a variety of situations.

E.g., volunteer with a non-profit organization, take a continuing education class, and participate in a new sport. When a man approaches you in one venue, invite him to do the other activities with you. If you met him in a business computers night class, suggest that he join you volunteering with Habitat For Humanity on Saturday, or at a rock climbing class on Sunday.

He'll see you using a variety of emotions. You may be confident and professional in the business computers class, caring and nurturing with the non-profit organization, and scared—then triumphant—climbing a cliff.

HOW OUR ANCESTORS LIVED

If human existence were as long as two copies of *Hearts And Minds*, for all but the last page of the second book—10,000 years —humans lived in small bands of hunter-gatherers. Archaeologists call this era the Paleolithic, or "early Stone Age."

Idyllic Lifestyle

The hunter-gatherer lifestyle is better than agricultural society in many ways. Hunter-gatherers moved around. They saw new vistas and ate different foods. Most appealing, they met other groups of people. In contrast, farmers are stuck in one place all their lives.

Hunter-gatherer diets were nutritious. They ate a wide variety of meat, fish, and plants. For example, the Yupic natives of coastal Alaska ate more than thirty species of mammals, birds, fish, and shellfish.[57] Starvation wasn't an issue in places with multiple food sources.

In contrast, agricultural diets are mostly corn, potatoes, wheat, or rice. These starchy foods lack protein, vitamins, and minerals. Better diets made our hunter-gatherer ancestors bigger (with bigger brains) than many modern people.

Men enjoyed hunting. They skillfully crafted weapons. They roamed far from home. They used intelligence to find animals. They used speed and strength to kill.

Women enjoyed socializing while gathering plants, snaring small game, and preparing food. Their children played around them, or stayed in camp with their elderly relatives.

Hunter-gatherers had many hours of leisure. Climates that required minimal shelter and clothing had little of the "housework" of our culture. In harsh climates, people could do little in the winter or during storms.

Small populations lived in large areas. Contagious diseases were unlikely to spread. Changing camps—before waste accumulated—

stopped endemic diseases.

Many cultures describe their ancestors as coming from an idyllic Garden of Eden or "land of milk and honey." These ancestral memories may be true.[58]

The Roman Cornelius Tacitus described a hunter-gatherer tribe in first-century Lithuania, as

> astonishingly savage and disgustingly poor. They have no proper weapons, no horses, no homes. They eat wild herbs....The women support themselves by hunting, exactly like the men....Yet they count their lot happier than that of others who groan over field labor.[59]
> — Tacitus, *Germania* (circa A.D. 100)

People continue to live as hunter-gatherers in northern Canada, the Australian outback, and central Africa. Contemporary hunter-gatherers live only on land that no one else wants, e.g., deserts, jungles, or frozen tundra. Their lives are difficult not because they're hunter-gatherers, but because they live on the worst land. 10,000 years ago, our ancestors lived good lives on abundant, temperate lands.

Egalitarian Groups

Hunter-gatherers were egalitarian. A large animal has more meat than one family can eat. A hunter loses nothing by giving away the extra meat to other families. When the hunter comes home empty-handed, he can expect other men to share their kills. Because hunter-gatherers can't store meat, they measure wealth by social connections.[60]

Hunter-gatherers couldn't accumulate wealth. They couldn't store food. They didn't build permanent houses. Each person owned only what he could carry.

With nothing to steal, violence was minimal and warfare nonexistent.

Men and women were equally responsible for producing food. They had equal status in hunter-gatherer societies. Hunter-gatherer societies have fixed gender roles, but everyone learns all basic skills for survival.

Each individual had equal opportunities to speak to the group. Each individual made his own decisions. A band that disagreed about a decision could split into two groups.[61]

Older people were libraries of knowledge, before the invention of writing. A band with an old woman might survive a flood or a drought, because she remembered what people did when a similar disaster happened decades earlier.

Children learned by observing adults, not through rote learning. Adults raised children to think independently. Children had to survive in case of disaster or separation from the group. Because hunter-gatherers live in small bands, boys and girls play together and behave more alike than children in larger societies.[62]

Limited Polygyny

Most hunter-gatherers were monogamous. Most hunters could provide only enough meat for one wife and her children. The best hunters could support two wives (polygyny).

Tacitus described a Neolithic (late Stone Age) German tribe as having

> One wife apiece—all of them except a very few who take more than one not to satisfy their desires, but because their exalted rank brings many pressing offers of matrimonial alliances. The dowry is brought by husband to wife...gifts [such as] oxen, a horse and bridle, or a shield, spear and sword...she in turn brings a present of arms to her husband....The woman must not think that she is excluded from aspirations to manly virtues or exempt from the hazards of warfare....She enters her husband's home to be the partner of his toils and perils, that both in peace and war she is to share his sufferings and adventures.... Clandestine love-letters are unknown to men and women alike. Adultery is extremely rare....Girls too are not hurried into marriage. As old and full-grown as the men they match their mates in age and strength.[63]
> — Tacitus, *Germania* (circa A.D. 100)

Were Our Ancestors Monogamous or Polygamous?

Biological and anthropological evidence suggests that our ancestral mothers were mildly polyandrous, i.e., women had more than one male sexual partner per birth.

Female gorillas are monogamous. Gorilla testes are one-quarter of the size of human testes (adjusted for body size). In contrast, female chimpanzees average 13 male sex partners per birth. Chimpanzee testes are three times the size of human testes (adjusted for body size). The size of human testes suggests that our ancestral mothers had several male sexual partners per birth.

As noted on page 9, the Aché hunter-gatherers are moderately polyandrous, with each child having, on average, 2.1 possible fathers.[64]

Biological and anthropological evidence also suggests that our ancestors were mildly polygynous, i.e., that men fathered children with more than one woman. In polygynous species, e.g., gorillas, males are bigger than females (*sexual dimorphism*). Males that win fights with other males mate with several females. Male gorillas are twice the size of females. In contrast, among monogamous species, e.g., gibbons, small males breed as often as large males. Gibbon males and females are the same size.

Men are somewhat larger than women, suggesting mild polygyny. This biological and anthropological evidence for polyandry and polygyny suggest that our ancestors were moderately polygamous (men with more than one woman and women with more than one man).[65]

Agricultural Societies

Agriculture started about 10,000 years ago. Women planted wild wheat and barley seeds near their camps, so they wouldn't have to walk far to collect grain. But someone had to stay and protect the crops from animals and other people. At first, elderly individuals did this. They spent their time making pottery containers to store grain.

Hunter-gatherer women could carry only one child. They

spaced children about four years apart, because a four-year-old could walk all day. Women married as adults, strong enough to carry a child.

In contrast, agricultural women didn't have to carry their children everywhere. They spaced children a year or two apart, producing larger families. Teenage girls married and reproduced before they were full-grown.

Agriculture and bigger families caused a vicious circle of increased food, but also increased population.[66] More labor had to go into working the fields, to produce enough food to feed everyone. More men had to farm. Fewer men hunted.

Individuals in agricultural societies became specialized. Some individuals did nothing but make pottery. Others became blacksmiths, shepherds, or soldiers. Specialization increased productivity, but population increases kept pace. Successive generations didn't live better.

Animal Husbandry and the Origins of Wealth

Farmers owned land. Some land was better than other land. Farmers owned plows and other tools for farming. They owned pottery and buildings for storing food. They built permanent houses, living in one place for generations.

Domesticated animals became an additional source of wealth. Dogs and pigs first came into camps to eat garbage. Children raised baby animals after hunters killed the animals' mothers. Farmers first raised domesticated animals for meat. Over time, men figured out how to harness large animals to plow fields, and to produce milk and wool.[67]

A man who owned a pair of sheep, cattle, or hogs soon had more livestock. A shepherd can watch one hundred sheep as easily as he can watch ten sheep. *Economies of scale* become possible. Some men became rich—and poor men became their slaves.[68]

Livestock made violence a profitable way of life. Stealing cattle was easy, especially for men skilled as hunters. For the first time, people owned a resource worth stealing. Cattle raids led to killing people, which led to warfare.[69]

Marriage and Divorce

Wealthy men supported larger families. Their wives spent more time producing children, and less time working outside the home. High-status men in agricultural societies had dozens or even hundreds of wives. Because high-status men had so many wives, many subordinate males had no wives or children.

Hunter-gatherer societies accepted divorce. Because individuals own only what they can carry, it's easy to split up. Divorce was economically impossible for farmers. A couple with fields, a house, and a barn couldn't divide the property in half. The individual who wanted out of the marriage had to leave empty-handed.[70]

Many immigrants to the United States and its western frontier were men leaving their marriages and land, looking for new land and new marriages.[71]

Negative Patterns

By the Neolithic era, we see the negative patterns of our own culture:

- A few wealthy, powerful men.
- Many poor, powerless men.
- Women valued for their ability to produce children, not for their minds.
- Women confined to their homes.
- Teenage girls marrying before reaching physical and intellectual maturity.
- Malnourishment in the best of times. Corn, wheat, potatoes, etc. don't provide balanced nutrition. Starvation in years of drought, flood, insects, etc.
- Many people living in close quarters spread diseases.
- Shorter lifespans, due to malnutrition and disease.
- Long hours of specialized, repetitive, mind-numbing work.
- War with neighboring tribes.
- Violence between bachelor men.
- Children disciplined into obedience, punished for independent thinking, and rewarded for working quietly in a group.
- Lack of support for teenagers' needs to feel that they are

unique, special individuals. Punishment of teenagers who assert their individuality.

- Old women became useless and disrespected, as books replaced them as sources of knowledge.
- Poor self-esteem. It's easier to make people work like slaves if they believe they're slaves. A philosopher observed, "The remarkable thing isn't that some men are slaves. The remarkable thing is that some men believe that they're slaves."[72]

Hunter-gatherer societies encouraged some individuals to develop transcendent abilities, e.g., prescience, communication with a spirit world, or physical feats such as firewalking. Speculatively, transcendent abilities could develop in the pre-frontal lobes of the cerebral cortex. Only humans have pre-frontal lobes. This is the most recent brain area to evolve, and, between the ages 15 to 21, the last to develop in each individual (see "Emotional Connection," page 14). A young person who receives support and guidance from a mentor to develop transcendent experiences might develop pre-frontal lobe capabilities that would otherwise be lost. The institutional religions of the agricultural era may have set back brain evolution.[73]

Cities and Civilization

Cities developed about 5,000 years ago. Civilization increased social stratification—i.e., the rich became richer, and the poor became poorer.

Village leaders became warlords, then kings, then emperors. Military organizations dominated regions, instead of occasionally raiding a neighboring village.

When primate brain size is compared to the number of animals in social groups, and then extrapolated to human brain size, humans appear to be hardwired for living in groups of about 155 individuals. If we live in a larger community, we put people into groups instead of thinking of them as individuals. I.e., communities of less than 155 individuals don't have "us and them" thinking.

On the positive side, civilization enabled new ideas to spread faster. New ideas breed more new ideas. Competitive individuals try to outsmart each other—making everyone smarter.

> A critical mass of people with such knowledge can multiply growth still further—essentially by creating knowledge clusters in which generally like-minded people bounce ideas off each other and compete. This dynamic is one reason why incomes are higher in cities than in rural areas and why nations that are already technologically advanced will quickly become more so.[74]
>
> — Bruce Bartlett

Industrial-Information Society

We're living in a third era. The Industrial-Information Age began in 1437, when Johannes Gutenberg invented the printing press.

Better information enabled technological advances—and, in a virtuous circle, technological advances produced better information.

Improved communication enabled oppressed peoples to organize themselves against autocratic rulers. Examples of liberation movements range from the American (1775–1783) and French Revolutions (1789–1795) to the civil rights movement of the 1960s and the women's movement of the 1970s.

Democracy vs. Women

Democratic revolutionaries replaced aristocracy. The Declaration of Independence, written by Thomas Jefferson, stated, "all men are created equal."[75] Jefferson intentionally excluded women.

> This new United States government was going to be the opposite of a court. All of the things that are features of court life—like kings, and absolute power, and courtiers, and the interplay of personal interests, and face-to-face politicking, and *influential women*—all of those things became anathema to the founders of this brand-new republic. Thomas Jefferson, who had been an ambassador in France, had particularly seen those court women ruling and having control over all kinds of official business, and he loathed it.[76]
>
> — Catherine Allgor, *Parlor Politics* (2000)

Instead, Jefferson envisioned an open government, with no behind-the-scenes politicking—and no women.[77]

The revolutionaries took power from the old rulers—the few powerful men, and most women. They gave power to the powerless—the majority of men. The United States didn't allow women to vote until 1920. Switzerland gave women the vote in 1970. Women aren't allowed to vote today in Saudi Arabia.

Hunter-Gatherer Values in the Industrial-Information Age

The industrial-information age enables us to return to our hunter-gatherer instincts.

In hunter-gatherer groups, everyone was economically equal. No individual owned more than he could carry. Today, poor Americans enjoy the standard of living—as measured by cars, televisions, air conditioners, etc.—that the middle-class enjoyed a generation ago.[78]

Hunter-gatherer groups had minimal violence. Violent crime is dropping in the United States. Fewer international conflicts occur. By 2100, violence and war may be rare.

In hunter-gatherer groups, men and women had equal status. Women's rights are among the achievements of the past 30 years.

Hunter-gatherers were mildly polygamous. We practice mild polygamy in the form of "serial monogamy." Like hunter-gatherers, we allow divorce.

Hunter-gatherers enjoyed seeing new scenery and meeting new people. Today, working class men and women admire long-distance truckers. Professional class men and women enjoy travel to "unspoiled" third-world countries. We all increasingly appreciate social diversity and the natural environment.

Delayed Reproduction to Reduce Overpopulation

Men should have their sperm frozen before 35, and wait until 40 or 45 to start a family. Women should wait until 30.

Older couples have the maturity for long-term committed relationships. They have the emotional maturity to raise children. Our descendants won't see dysfunctional families as normal.

Older couples have accumulated wealth. At least one parent doesn't have to work. Our descendants will see two working parents as barbaric.

Couples that marry later are less likely to divorce. Children without fathers don't develop their brains' masculine hardwiring. Future generations will view single parenting as barbaric.

Delayed reproduction reduces population growth. If a 32-year-old woman and her 44-year-old husband have two children, and the parents live to 76, population growth is zero. In contrast, a 19-year-old couple with two children increases the population *seven-fold*—when such a couple dies, two children, four grandchildren, and eight great-grandchildren replace them.

Effects of Television on Children's Brain Development

Before television, children listened to adults telling stories. Imagining a story stimulated a child's cerebral cortex. Vicariously feeling the adult's emotions stimulated the child's limbic brain. Acting out a story (a central activity in Waldorf schools) integrates the reptilian brain, limbic brain, and cerebral cortex.

In contrast, television provides visual and auditory stimulation, leaving nothing for the child to imagine. Children become emotionally attached to television actors, but the emotions are one-way (i.e., the actors don't love the children). Sitting still doesn't develop a child's reptilian brain.

One hundred years ago, doctors espousing the new germ theory of disease told mothers not to touch their infants. Fifty years ago, doctors told mothers not to breastfeed. Many of these infants died. The surviving infants didn't receive the emotional relationships needed for limbic brain development.[79] To future generations, allowing children to watch television may seem as barbaric as not allowing mothers to touch or feed their infants.[80]

MONOGAMY AND POLYGAMY

Judging from the social habits of man as he now exists, and from most savages being polygamists, the most probable view is that primeval man aboriginally lived in small communities, each with as many wives as he could support and obtain, whom he would have jealously guarded against all other men.[81]
— Charles Darwin, *The Descent of Man* (1871)

About 85% of human societies are *polygynous*, in which some men marry more than one wife.[82] Only 15% of societies are strictly monogamous. No societies are *polyandrous*, in which one woman marries several husbands (not counting extramarital sex, and a poor region of India and Tibet where women marry brothers because the work of several men is needed to provide resources to raise a family). Only 3% of mammal species are monogamous.[83]

In historical terms, it is monogamy that is in need of explanation, not polygamy.[84]
— Janet Bennion, *Women of Principle* (1998)

Women—Egalitarian Sisterhood

Imagine a society in which the only wealth is cattle. A village has 1000 men, 1000 women, and 1000 cows.

The Grand Pooh-bah has 100 wives and 100 cows. The Lieutenant Pooh-bah has three wives and three cows. Some men have one wife and one cow. Most men have no wife or cow.

In this society, every woman has one husband and one cow. All women are equal. Most men suffer in this society.

In a polygynous society, the median woman is better off than the median man. The wives of wealthy, monogamous men may object to this statement—until their husbands divorce them for younger women.

Men, on average, are better off in a monogamous society. All men have equal opportunities for a wife and family. It's ironic that men, whose sexuality is more polygynous than women's sexuality, are the beneficiaries of monogamy.

Women's Power

In a *kyriarchical* society, a few powerful men subjugate everyone else (from the Greek *kyri* or dominant lord[85]). Women's preference for high-status men produced these societies. If women believed all men to be equally attractive, human societies would be egalitarian.

In kyriarchical societies, women made most decisions. A warlord couldn't trust other men, because they'd usurp his power. He left day-to-day decision making with his senior wives. I.e., matriarchy and kyriarchy are closely related.

E.g., from 1981 to 1985, the Indian guru Bhagwan Shree Rajneesh (later named Osho, see photo page 192) was the "alpha" male of his Oregon community. He lay around his trailer on Valium and nitrous oxide. Seven women ran the community. These "alpha" women poisoned 751 residents of a nearby town, in an attempt to control local elections. No evidence indicated that the Bhagwan was involved in the attack.[86]

A five-year study of a polygynist religious fundamentalist community in Montana found

> that women are actually *drawn* to the group, voluntarily —and in significant numbers—and that men are not the key players in the management of domestic activities and community welfare, as has always been assumed. Women are the key players.[87]
> — Janet Bennion, *Women of Principle* (1998)

The study concludes by "identifying female solidarity as a key to female status, satisfaction, and power."[88] Women are happiest and strongest when they have close, supportive relationships with other women.

Increasing Status via Hypergamy

In ancestral societies, high-status wives had economic resources. They were physically protected. Most important, their son might become the next Grand Pooh-bah.

E.g., the Moroccan emperor Moulay Ismail the Bloodthirsty (c. 1672) had four wives, 500 concubines, and 888 children.[89] His mom won the genetic lottery. Her genes passed on to 888 grandchildren.

In a society ruled by kinship (as opposed to written laws), polygyny creates alliances between families. Marriages increase community stability.[90] Recall from the last chapter why Late Neolithic leaders were polygynous:

> not to satisfy their desires, but because their exalted rank brings many pressing offers of matrimonial alliances.[91]
> — Tacitus, *Germania* (circa A.D. 100)

In a class-stratified society, polygyny enables women (but not men) to move up. Attractive young women from low-status families marry high-status men.[92]

> Women are encouraged to practice "hypergamy," or marrying up, to…a man who holds a high spiritual or priesthood rank [these men are usually financially better-off too]…women in this type of system, ideally, gain a better status through marrying the elite of the group, while men marry downward.[93]
> — Janet Bennion, *Women of Principle* (1998)

In polygynous societies, men pay *bridewealth* for wives. A wealthy man can marry as many women as he can support. Bridewealth redistributes wealth from rich families to poor families —or at least to poor families with attractive daughters. Bridewealth increases social equality. Daughters are valued as potential wealth and upward mobility.

In monogamous societies, parents pay men *dowry* to marry their daughters. The family buys the highest-status husband they can afford. They pay the husband to be monogamous. Dowries increase social stratification. Rich families become richer, especially if they have more sons than daughters. Daughters are unwanted financial and social liabilities.

Careers vs. Motherhood

In a polygynous society, one wife can focus on her career while another wife raises their children:

> As a journalist, I work many unpredictable hours in a fast-paced environment. The news determines my schedule. But am I calling home, asking my husband to please pick up the kids and pop something in the microwave and get them to bed on time just in case I'm really late? Because of my plural marriage arrangement, I don't have to worry. I know that when I have to work late my daughter will be at home surrounded by loving adults.... My eight-year-old has never seen the inside of a day-care center, and my husband has never eaten a TV dinner. And I know that when I get home from work, if I'm dog-tired and stressed-out, I can be alone and guilt-free. It's a rare day when all eight of my husband's wives are tired and stressed at the same time.[94]
> — Elizabeth Joseph, "Polygamy: The Ultimate Feminist Lifestyle"

Men—Masters, Slaves, and Welfare Cheats

The average American polygynist man has three or four wives. Wives average eight children. Men average 28 children.[95]

If a man financially supports his families (most polygynous American men don't), he has to work long hours, instead of spending time with his family.

> For men...any sexual motives must surely pall after a while, as the day-to-day pressures of plural family life cumulate—the financial burdens, the needs of large families, family tensions and conflicts, and so on....plural family life is not especially "romantic" for men.[96]
> — Irwin Altman and Joseph Ginat, Polygamous Families in Contemporary Society (1996)

If a polygynous man cares whether his four wives and 28 children get along with each other, he has to follow almost one thousand relationships. Morality is how people relate to each other. If a man doesn't pay attention to the relationships within his family, he doesn't care about his family's morality.

Class Stratification

In the Montana polygynist community, one-third of the converts eventually left. Three out of four who left were male.[97] Community stratification dissatisfied these men.

To convert, men give money, land, and possessions to the community. Men have to go through religious and character tests. After converting, men are at the bottom of the hierarchy. The elite men—mostly the sons of the founders—get marital, financial, and religious advantages.

Women have advantages at every stage of conversion. The community doesn't ask women to contribute wealth. They believe that women are inherently more virtuous. Women pass the religious tests more easily.

Women are encouraged to marry high-status men, to immediately join the community elite. Women converts are *ten times* more likely to integrate into the upper class than men converts.

Incest, Child Abuse, and Wife Battering

When a handful of men have absolute power, expect absolute corruption. Another polygynous community has a reputation for incest, child abuse, and wife battering.[98]

In Colorado City, Arizona, men in their 40s, 50s, 60s, and even 70s barter their 15-year-old daughters. The more girls a man gives away to his friends, the more girls he gets in return.[99] These aren't relationships between consenting adults.

Warren Jeffs, the Colorado City religious leader, ordered parents not to send their children to school:[100]

> A child that's not in school is a child that can't tell a counselor they're being abused.[101]
>
> — Ron Allen, Utah state senator

Unlike the Montana community, most apostates (individuals who leave) are women.

Men often marry their stepsisters or cousins. Inbreeding, or old men's defective sperm, produces many children with disabilities.[102]

> Down's syndrome children are prized here for their docile nature and the fact that their families receive $500 a month from the government for their care.
>
> "You see these young pregnant mothers rubbing their stomachs saying, 'I hope this one's a Down's,'" said Eunice Bateman, a former plural wife.
>
> Rowenna Erickson, a former plural wife, calls the health care for children in polygamy a "freak show," saying pregnant women seldom receive prenatal care.[103]
>
> — Julie Cart, *Los Angeles Times* (2001)

Welfare Fraud

Welfare fraud supports families. Polygynous wives tell state agencies that they're single. Colorado City residents receive *eight times* more government services than they pay in taxes.[104] *Every* school-age child lives below the poverty level.[105]

Tom Green has five wives and thirty children. Utah convicted him of criminal nonsupport and welfare fraud. He and his wives fraudulently obtained $150,000 in welfare benefits.[106] The state also charged him with child rape, after marrying a 13-year-old girl. The state sentenced Green to five years in prison.

> Some men seem to be using their religion as an excuse for behavior that shouldn't be tolerated.[107]
> — Ron Barton, Utah state investigator

Violence in Polygynous Societies

Polygynous societies are more violent than monogamous societies.

Polygynous societies have more single men than single women. The competition for scarce women can be brutal, sometimes lethal. Murderers are three times more likely to be single than married.[108]

Judaism, Christianity, Islam, and Polygyny

In the Old Testament, the patriarchs Abraham, Jacob, David, and Solomon were polygynous.[109]

Deuteronomy 25:5–6 requires men to marry their brothers' widows, as second wives. Polygyny wasn't about promiscuous sex, but rather was a duty to care for widows and orphans.

> **Polygamy, as ideally practiced, is more Christian than divorce and remarriage as far as the abandoned wives and children are concerned.**[110]
> — Father Eugene Hillman, *Polygamy Reconsidered*
> (1975)

The Jewish Talmud limits a man to four wives. European Jews practiced polygyny until the sixteenth century. Jews in Yemen continue to practice polygyny.[111]

In the New Testament, Paul opposed marriage. He followed the Stoic philosophy that marriage and children distract from religious devotion.

In contrast, Judaism and Islam value marriage as the ideal state for most people. In these societies, polygyny is an ideal form of marriage—if the husband has the resources to provide for his wives, and the good character to raise children.

In A.D. 393, the Pope reversed the Deuteronomy levirate. The Pope adapted Christianity to Roman law, which forbade polygyny, but allowed prostitution and concubines (concubines were wives whose children didn't inherit the father's wealth—we call them—ironically—*mistresses*).[112]

The Koran (A.D. 651) requires that prosperous men marry destitute widows. The husband must raise the widow's children as his own. A man may marry up to four women.[113]

Marriage and divorce were central issues in the sixteenth-century Protestant reformation. Martin Luther believed that ministers should marry. England's King Henry VIII loved Anne Boleyn, but was married to Catherine of Aragon. Henry asked Pope Clement VII to annul his marriage. The Pope refused. Henry then declared the Church of England independent of Rome—the first large nation to become Protestant.

Charismatic Protestant rebel leaders often found themselves surrounded by adoring female converts—and declared that the Old Testament allows polygyny. Polygyny in these sects always died out within a generation—sometimes by burning at the stake.[114]

Contemporary Monogamy and Polygamy

> When [my husband] told me, "The sign that I'd had an affair was a sign that there's something wrong in our relationship," I thought, "No Frenchman would ever have said that."
>
> It's a given that in a long relationship there will be an affair somewhere along the road, for both partners, not just for men, so it would not be interpreted as a sign that there's something wrong.
>
> I think Americans are more idealist, a sense of purity and innocence. If people fall in love, and they truly love each other, then there will be no other people in their lives, and they will be monogamous for fifty years. The French would laugh at that concept.
>
> I'm not saying that it's easy to live the Parisian style, but I think it's more realistic. It's less idealistic, it's making room for reality, there are temptations, there are other men and women we encounter along the road.[115]
>
> — Catherine Texier, *Breakup: The End of a Love Story*
> (1998)

Biologists describe a species as monogamous if the animals

1) Raise their young together.
2) Stay together for life.

Most monogamous species are less promiscuous than other species. However, all animals will have sex with an animal other than his or her mate if the opportunity arises.[116]

By these standards, American "serial monogamy" is polygamy. In contrast, the French—who accept extramarital sex—are monogamous.

Men's and Women's Desired Number of Partners

72% of men said yes when an attractive female stranger asked to have sex. All women said no when propositioned by an attractive male stranger.[117]

Men, on average, want six partners in the next year, and 18 in their lifetimes.[118] In reality, 23% of American men have had two or more sexual partners in the past year. The average man has about five sexual partners in his lifetime.[119]

Women want one sexual partner in the next year, and four in their lifetimes.[120] In reality, 12% had two or more partners—half the number of men with two or more partners.[121] The average woman has 3.5 sex partners in her lifetime.[122]

In other words, women, on average, get the number of partners they want. Men, on average, don't.

When Masculine Sexuality Is Acceptable

Feminine sexuality (long-term monogamous relationships) is the norm in all societies. But all societies allow masculine sexuality (sex with many partners) somewhere, sometimes, or for some individuals. Each society has different rules about this. E.g., in Italian coastal villages, young men can have sex with foreign tourist women, but not with local women.

To use masculine sexuality, follow your community's rules, move to a community that has rules you like, or hope you have enough cerebral cortex to break the rules without getting caught.

Stress and Promiscuity

When our ancestral mothers felt secure, they chose feminine sexuality and monogamous relationships. But in times of life-threatening stress (e.g., famine or war), women who traded sex for food or safety (i.e., switched to masculine sexuality) survived and became our ancestral mothers.

Physical abuse (one form of life-threatening stress) makes teenage girls six times more likely to have risky, promiscuous sex. Witnessing parental fights, but not being abused, makes teenage girls three times more likely to have risky, promiscuous sex.[123]

Teenage girls from troubled families are more sexually active, at earlier ages, and are more likely to become pregnant.[124] Divorce, lack of support from their fathers, or "male bashing" mothers cause teenage girls to believe that men are unnecessary for raising children.[125] I.e., teenage girls become promiscuous because they *don't* value men.

Conversely, girls who develop secure attachments to both parents, and grow up in a low-stress home, later delay sexual intercourse and choose long-term, stable mates.[126] I.e., women who most love men love the fewest men; women who least love men love the most men.

Affectionate relationships between girls and their biological fathers delay puberty. The most important period for this effect is the first five years of the girls' lives. Close relationships with mothers are less significant for pubertal delay. The opposite effect is seen when girls have close relationships with unrelated males, e.g., stepfathers.[127] This effect may be related to pheromones.

Some individuals handle stress poorly (see "Confidence and Stress," page 10). A woman who handles stress poorly is more likely to become promiscuous, in situations that another woman easily handles. Men who abuse women cause stress to women and see how they react. If a woman confidently handles the problem, the man leaves her alone. If she handles stress poorly, he recognizes a potential victim.

Smoking, alcohol, and drug use signal inability to handle stress, and subsequent promiscuity. Substance abuse causes daily stress (e.g., getting a fix, or hiding an addiction).

> At age nineteen…15 percent of nonsmoking white women attending college have had sex. The same number for white female college students who do smoke is 55 percent. The statistics for men are about the same.[128]
> — Malcolm Gladwell, *The Tipping Point* (2000)

Sexual Satisfaction in Monogamous Relationships

The best sex is within marriages.[129] 86% of married men and women say they're very or extremely satisfied with their sex lives.[130]

75% of individuals in monogamous relationships who live alone say they're very or extremely satisfied with their sex lives.

Of individuals with two sexual partners, only 70% say they're very or extremely satisfied with their primary sex partner. Satisfaction with the secondary partner averages only 44%.[131] I.e., the grass isn't greener on the other side of the fence.

Married men and women are also happier. Twice as many single individuals suffer from stress, compared to married individuals (25% vs. 13%). Married men and married women have the same stress levels, on average.[132]

Is There a "Marriage Crisis"?

In 1970, the divorce rate was 33% of the marriage rate, i.e., one-third of marriages ended in divorce. By 1991, the divorce rate had climbed to 50%.[133]

However, the median duration of marriage increased from 6.7 years in 1970 to 7.2 years in 1990.[134]

These contradictory trends were due to several factors. First, life expectancy increased from 70.8 in 1970 to 75.4 in 1990.[135] People now live longer, and marry longer.

Another factor is cohabitation. Fewer couples marry now, but more live together. The marriage rate declined, but the "monogamy rate" (including serial monogamy) remains the same.

A third factor was a relative shortage of men born between 1933 and 1957 (see "Man Shortage or Commitment Shortage?" page 95).

Serial Monogamy Tends Toward Polyandry

Judging from women's clothing, contemporary Americans are *polyandrous*. Polygynous species—in which a male has sex with many females—are identified by males' brightly colored feathers, long tails, huge antlers, etc. The males look sexy, to attract females. The females are drab, to camouflage their nests from predators.

Until 200 years ago, aristocratic men looked sexy in brightly colored silks and satins, lace, tights, and high-heeled, pointy-toed shoes. Aristocratic men were polygynous, if you count mistresses and servants. Aristocratic women's large dresses displayed wealth, but hid their bodies.

The French revolution (1789–1795) made aristocracy unpopular (and sometimes lethal). Men's clothing became drab and functional.[136] After a brief period of simplicity, women's clothing returned to displaying wealth, while hiding their bodies.[137]

World War One (1914–1918) killed 37 million young men.[138] In the 1920s, women competed for men. Women's clothes became sexy. Hemlines rose and necklines fell.

Couples married young in the 1950s. Married women didn't need to compete for men. Women went back to hiding their bodies in large dresses.

The divorce rate started to increase in the 1960s. Older women outnumber older men, so they have to look sexy to attract a partner (or to keep a husband from having affairs with younger women). Serial monogamy becomes polyandry as women age. Older women buy sexy clothes, but want to see it advertised on young models. (*Playboy* bizarrely dresses young women in clothes—well, in high-heeled shoes—that only women over 50 would buy.)

Young women avoid sexy clothes, except in movies and magazines, or for a special night out (usually with their girlfriends). Young women prefer oversize sweatshirts, jeans, and big boots or comfortable sandals. Young women, like females of other species, dress to avoid attention.

African-American Marriage and Polygyny

In 1970, white Americans and African-Americans had similar marriage rates.[139] In the 1990s, the marriage rate for African-Americans was one-half to one-third the marriage rate for white Americans.[140] E.g., half of African-American women will never marry, compared to one-sixth of white American women.[141]

Marital satisfaction among African-Americans is lower than among whites.[142] The divorce rate is higher.[143]

Many African-American men are underemployed,[144] addicted to alcohol or other drugs, or in prison.[145] These factors make them less likely to marry.

Many African-American women are on welfare. Women on

welfare are less likely to marry.[146] The modern welfare system began in the late 1960s.[147] The decline of African-American marriage matched the rise of welfare. Compare our welfare system to that of the Bible and the Koran (see "Judaism, Christianity, Islam, and Polygyny," page 45), in which marriage is the institution through which prosperous families help poor families.

Some successful, married African-American men secretly support a single mother, in return for sex. Typically, the woman has children from previous relationships. She then has another child with her benefactor.

> A woman's comment that we needed to learn from Africa where polygamy was responsibly practiced, elicited widespread applause from both men and women. One man spoke to the crux of the issue when he stated that society's moral level overall needed to be raised because there is no reason to expect men to act better if we get polygamy without an improvement in morality.[148]
> — Philip Kilbride, *Plural Marriage For Our Times* (1994)

The good news is that an African-American woman can increase her likelihood to marry by getting an education and a career[149] (see "Education and Employment," page 27)—and attending church doubles her likelihood to marry.[150]

HORMONES

Testosterone

Testosterone is a hormone produced primarily in men's testes. The adrenal glands of both men and women also produce small amounts of testosterone.[151]

In men, testosterone produces sperm, facial and body hair, deep voices, and muscle mass and strength.[152]

Testosterone is associated with two behaviors in males: aggressive dominance of other males, and sexual activity. E.g., male red deer live peacefully together for most of the year. But in October their testosterone increases five-fold. They fight for territory. Female red deer select land that has sufficient food for raising fawns. The males that control the best territories mate with the most females.[153]

Testosterone is an anti-depressant.[154] It increases friendliness. It reduces anger, depression, fatigue, confusion, nervousness, and irritability.[155]

That may seem contradictory—testosterone makes males fight, yet makes them friendly. Testosterone makes males want to mate. If fighting precedes mating—e.g., gorillas—testosterone makes males fight. But if mating requires friends—e.g., baboons—testosterone makes males friendly.

Testosterone and Sexual Behavior
Testosterone is necessary for sexual activity. However, the amount of testosterone needed for sexual activity is low.[156] Testosterone injections don't increase sexual activity or sexual desire in young men.[157] Men have more than enough testosterone for sex.

Who Has the Most Testosterone?
Testosterone varies between men more than four times.[158] Football players have the most testosterone. Ministers have the least.[159]

Men and women with high testosterone commit more violent crimes. They're more unruly in prison. Parole boards judge them more harshly.[160]

Bachelors have more testosterone than married men. Childless husbands have more testosterone than fathers.[161] Low testosterone in men correlates with marital satisfaction. Low testosterone improves emotional expressiveness, parent-child communication, and "androgynous behaviors"—the ability to use feminine skills when necessary.[162]

Testosterone in Women

Women have about one-tenth of men's testosterone.[163] If you don't believe that women have testosterone, watch *Girlfight* (2000), starring Michelle Rodriguez.

Women's sexuality requires testosterone.[164] Women with more testosterone have less depression, more sexual enjoyment, better interpersonal relationships, and happier marriages.[165] Happy marriages consist of high-testosterone women and low-testosterone men.

Women executives and attorneys have more testosterone than secretaries, teachers, nurses, and housewives.[166]

Women who don't use condoms are less depressed than women who use condoms, or who aren't sexually active. Women who don't use condoms become increasingly depressed as time elapses since their last sexual encounter. They also seek new partners sooner after ending a relationship. Women apparently absorb an anti-depressant hormone, possibly testosterone, from semen.[167]

If you're a depressed woman, talk to your doctor about trying a low dosage of testosterone instead of Prozac or other anti-depressants.

Alcohol and Testosterone

Alcohol lowers men's testosterone. Liver damage (associated with alcoholism) increases clearance of testosterone from the blood. Liver damage decreases clearance of estrogen.[168] Increased estrogen and decreased testosterone reduce the functioning of men's testes.

Alcohol has no effect on the hormones of healthy non-alcoholic young women.[169] Alcoholism reduces sexual functioning in women, but not as severely as the effect in men.[170]

Boost Your Testosterone Without Pills or Patches
To boost your testosterone:
- Avoid alcohol, if you're a man.
- Sexual activity increases testosterone, in both men and women.[171]
- Winning boosts testosterone. Losing reduces testosterone. Find a sport you can win at, e.g., softball vs. baseball. You have to win at something indicative of social dominance, e.g., winning the lottery doesn't affect testosterone.[172]
- The presence of females boosts male testosterone. New females especially boost testosterone.[173] Speculatively, young women increase men's testosterone more than older women. You don't need to have sex to get this effect. The effect is produced via pheromones in women's sweat. Play a sport you can win, on a team with sweating young women.

Testosterone and Aging
Pre-pubescent boys have little testosterone. After puberty, testosterone increases in teenagers. Testosterone is generally stable until men are in their 60s. Testosterone then decreases in old age.[174] Diminishing testosterone doesn't sufficiently explain the declining sexual activity associated with aging.[175]

A study in the United States, Congo, Nepal, and Paraguay found that Americans have the highest testosterone when young, and the least in old age. Testosterone levels are nearly flat across lifespans in traditional societies.[176] This may be due to how American men and women interact. Young American men interact with many young women, in high school and college. Older American men have little interaction with non-related young women—or their secretaries wear anti-perspirant.

Estrogen and Progesterone

Women's ovaries produce *estrogen* and *progesterone*.[177] Estrogen increases in girls at puberty, making them develop breasts and hips. Estrogen drops at menopause (around age 50).

Estrogen is associated with ovulation and sexual receptivity. In female animals, estrogen increases male interest in the female,[178] female solicitations of males for sex,[179] and male sexual performance.[180]

Orgasms increase women's estrogen.[181]

Progesterone

Progesterone is associated with pregnancy, nursing, and other nonfertile states.[182]

Progesterone reduces female sexual behavior.[183] It inhibits orgasm.[184] It causes mild depression.[185] Prisons use a form of progesterone to "chemically castrate" male sex offenders.[186]

Progesterone increases maternal behavior. E.g., progesterone causes female rabbits to build nests.[187] Progesterone causes maternal aggression toward animals that approach a mother's young.[188]

A variety of behaviors affect progesterone. Breastfeeding,[189] oral contraceptives,[190] and lack of exercise[191] increase progesterone—and reduce sex drive.

Increased progesterone may be a factor in the 70% drop in marital satisfaction in the first few years after the birth of a couple's first child.[192]

Sexual Peaks of the Menstrual Cycle

Estrogen, progesterone, and testosterone vary widely over women's 28-day menstrual cycles (see Figure 2: Hormones Over Menstrual Cycle).

For the first 10–12 days after menstrual bleeding ceases, estrogen and testosterone are low but increasing. Progesterone is very low. A woman described this time as "confident and social, on the prowl."[193]

Women ovulate around days 13–15. Estrogen and testosterone

peak. Progesterone remains low. Brain scans show that women respond more dramatically to pictures of nude men during ovulation.[194] Sexual behavior peaks. Ovulating women in singles bars wear more jewelry and makeup. They have more physical contact with men.[195]

> You know "that look" women get when they want sex? Me neither.
>
> — Steve Martin

During the two weeks after ovulation, progesterone dominates. Estrogen remains moderately high. Testosterone diminishes. Progesterone makes women not want sex, but feel nurturing. A woman described this time as "too tired for an orgasm, but could have touched all night."[196]

Progesterone and estrogen drop a few days before menstruation. This relates to premenstrual syndrome (PMS) in some women.[197]

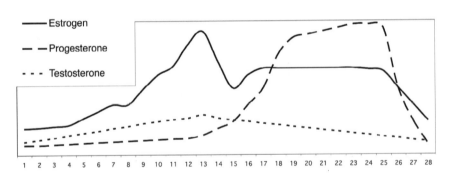

Figure 2: Hormones Over Menstrual Cycle

If you're a man reading this, you're thinking: "If I knew when women were ovulating, dating would be much easier!" Indeed, females of all other species show males when they're ovulating. Many species are physically incapable of intercourse when the female isn't ovulating.

But women *conceal ovulation*. If they didn't, men would date them when they were ovulating, and date other women the rest of the month. Women conceal ovulation to get their partners to pay attention to them every day. If a man doesn't know when his wife is fertile, he must have sex with her more or less every day of the month to father a child—or each day stop her from having sex with other men, to prevent other men from getting her pregnant.

Oxytocin

The pituitary gland (in the brain) produces *oxytocin*. Both males and females produce oxytocin. Oxytocin is unique to mammals.

Affectionate touching releases oxytocin. Cuddling a child or pet is pleasurable because of oxytocin. An infant suckling releases the mother's oxytocin, making nursing pleasurable for women.

Individuals who regularly cuddle can become addicted to each other. They can experience oxytocin withdrawal when apart.[198]

Oxytocin releases cyclically. Couples reach the highest levels of sexual feeling by alternating about twenty minutes of intense touching with relaxation or less intense touching.

Orgasm spikes oxytocin to five times normal levels. The *refractory* or disinterested period some people feel after sex may be due in part to oxytocin overdose (too much of any drug reduces sexual interest).[199] Test this hypothesis by cuddling more when you're not having sex, to get your brain used to oxytocin.[200]

Pheromones and MHC

We're hardwired to sense genetically similar individuals—i.e., our relatives—and give them friendship and support.[201] But we're hardwired for sexual attraction to opposite individuals.

Animals produce chemical *pheromones* to cause sexual, territorial, or other behaviors in another animal. The vomeronasal organ (VNO) in the nose detects pheromones. The VNO is distinct from the nose's smell faculty—pheromones are a "sixth" sense.

Parents with different immune systems produce offspring with strong immune systems. Parents with similar immune systems can be infertile or have miscarriages. Females sense a male's immune system via *major histocompatibility complex* (MHC) molecules.

The VNO appears to sense MHC.

The sweat of men with different MHC attracts women. The sweat of men with similar MHC repulses women. (Health clubs could offer smellable personal ads!)

The surprise is that women on birth control pills are attracted to men with similar MHC. Men with different MHC repulse them. Birth control pills make a woman's body think she's pregnant. Pregnant female animals seek males with similar MHC. These males are likely to be relatives and will protect their baby relations. A man who attracts a woman when she's not on the pill will repulse her if she goes on the pill.[202]

Pheromones Are Not Body Odor

Bacteria and fungi live on your skin and on your clothes. These little critters drink your sweat and eat your discarded skin cells. Their excretions make you smell disgusting. That's body odor.[203]

Women's sense of smell is better than men's. Ask a woman if you smell bad. If so, shower with antibacterial soap. If that doesn't eliminate B.O., shave your body hair, especially your armpits. Body hair holds body odor (head hair is different).

But frequent showering also washes away your pheromones. To attract women, men need pheromones *without* body odor. Contrary to spam e-mail advertisements, you can't buy human sexual pheromone colognes. Don't be afraid to sweat on a date, if you've gotten rid of skin bacteria.

Do Men and Women Have Different Sex Drives?

Men's sex drive results from one hormone. Testosterone varies 50% or more daily,[204] varies even more between men, and diminishes with age, but, compared to women, the male sex drive is relatively constant. In general, men are ready for sex anytime, anywhere, with any female.

In contrast, three hormones—estrogen, progesterone, and testosterone—control women's sex drive. Women's interest in sex varies in character and intensity over their menstrual cycles, during pregnancy and nursing, and during menopause. Women's sex drives can be as strong or stronger than men's, but only at specific times.

Females will have sex only in certain places. E.g., female elephant seals select a beach with minimal danger from predators. Female red deer select a meadow with abundant food to support fawns. Human females like vacation resorts with nice beaches and plenty of food.

Females prefer to mate with specific males. Whether a male physically dominated other males (e.g., gorillas), or built a social network (e.g., baboons), or is one's life partner (e.g., gibbons), rejecting inappropriate males is central to female sexuality.

Fetal Testosterone and Brain Differences

Fetuses are of "indifferent" sex for the first six weeks. Fetuses with XY (male) chromosomes then produce testosterone. Testosterone causes the XY fetus to develop male genitalia and physique.

XY fetuses convert some of the testosterone into estrogen. Estrogen masculinizes a fetus.[205]

XX (female) fetuses are normally not exposed to testosterone or estrogen. They develop feminine features, thinking, and behavior.

Cognitive Differences

Women generally have better senses of smell, taste, and hearing. Men generally have better vision.[206]

Women have better verbal skills. They have better fine motor skills, e.g., threading a needle. Men are better at "directed motor skills," e.g., throwing a ball, and "visual-spatial abilities," e.g., map reading and mental rotation of 3-D objects.[207]

Men use one brain area at a time. Men can concentrate on a task for long periods.[208] Focusing on an activity without distractions soothes men, e.g., driving a motorcycle across the country.

Women multi-task, e.g., minding a baby while cooking dinner while talking on the telephone. A "woman's intuition" results from using her whole brain to solve a problem.

Abnormal Fetal Testosterone

XX (female) fetuses exposed to testosterone develop masculinized features, e.g., a clitoris as large as a small penis, and masculine thinking patterns and behaviors. Conversely, XY (male) fetuses not exposed to testosterone become feminized.[209]

Switching the hormones of baby animals—rats, ferrets, pigs, finches, and monkeys[210]—makes males grow up to behave as females, and vice versa.[211] Females attempt to mount females. Males assume the *lordosis* female sexual posture to get males to mount them.[212] Given a choice of male or female sexual partners, the hormonally manipulated animals choose their own sex.[213]

Stressing pregnant rats (e.g., forcing them to remain immobile in bright light, which terrifies normally nocturnal animals) causes them to produce homosexual or bisexual male offspring.[214]

Some genetic disorders expose human XX (female) fetuses to testosterone or estrogen, or prevent testosterone exposure of XY (male) fetuses.[215] These XY (male) adults look and act like women (including sexual attraction to men). The XX (female) girls prefer to play with trucks instead of dolls.[216] The adult women have masculine features, behavior, and sexual attraction to women.[217]

Gender identity, gender role, sexual orientation, and cognitive skills appear to develop at different stages of pregnancy. Abnormal fetal hormones at certain points in pregnancy can produce one gender abnormality, while the individual otherwise develops normally. E.g., a man could think of himself as masculine, wear men's clothing, etc., but feel sexual attraction to other men.[218]

Abnormal fetal testosterone can be a gift. Normal men and women get stuck in masculine or feminine thinking patterns. Too often men can't understand women. Women can't understand men. But, as in the saying "two heads are better than one," gays and lesbians can solve problems that stump other men and women.[219] They can use masculine aggressiveness and goal-orientation. They can use feminine listening, verbal, and social skills. Gays and lesbians can be adept diplomats—or spies.

♥

COMMUNICATION STYLES

The Great Male Hierarchy

Women don't think that all men were created equal. In most species, females prefer to mate with certain males. Females' preferences created the Great Male Hierarchy.

Hierarchies have many advantages. Leaders provide for the welfare of men below them. Subordinate men support the leaders. Every man has a job to do. Leaders make and execute decisions quickly.

New men can join the hierarchy at any time—at the bottom. No time is wasted deciding who likes or dislikes whom.

"Ego boosts"—praise and appreciation that boosts a man up the hierarchy—can be more important than anything else.

> It is with baubles that battles are won.[220]
> — Napoleon Bonaparte, creating the Legion d'Honour
> medal

Conversely, fear of embarrassment—a fall down the hierarchy —makes soldiers risk their lives. An insult—a shove down the hierarchy—"drives a man to distraction" or makes him ignore more important goals.

The hierarchical model works with a dozen men, or a million men.

Men in a hierarchy have no need to put down any other man. They establish rules. The rule of law supplants force and violence. The organization runs smoothly. Courts and justice systems are hierarchies.

The downside of hierarchies is that high-status individuals can abuse low-status individuals.[221] A male hierarchy with thirty million members—e.g., Nazi Germany—has far more potential for abuse than a thirty-member women's circle.

Women's Support Circles

Women form egalitarian support circles. When a woman has a problem, the other women in her circle help her. This structure promotes sharing of resources. Support circles take care of each member.

Women compliment each other and put themselves down to say, "You're in my circle."

Instead of having set jobs, at different times individuals have different roles. A woman with resources or skills needed today helps her sisters. They'll care for her at another time.

Women play games to socialize. In contrast, men play to win.

The downside of women's support circles is that they're effective only up to about thirty members. Decisions require consensus. Women's circles can talk and talk and talk instead of making a decision.

Women in a circle exclude other women. Women gossip to say, "You're in my circle." Women make "catty" remarks to exclude individuals from their circle.

Only five women head Fortune 500 companies.[222] But few women are homeless. The top and bottom of the Great Male Hierarchy are far apart. Women's egalitarian instincts keep them from society's depths as well as its heights.

Men: "Report Talk"

Men communicate to establish social hierarchies:
- Putting each other down, showing off, or boasting.
- Talking about things they did, a.k.a. "report talk."
- Issuing orders or commands—"Bring me a beer!"
- "Anger as a greeting." A man makes a verbal challenge. If the other man stands up to him, they respect each other.
- Men disagree to show superiority. E.g., a man admires a Honda motorcycle. His buddy replies that Harley-Davidson motorcycles are better.
- Men refuse offers of help. This shows that a man is independent. Dependence indicates low status.
- Men find something positive in every situation. "No, I didn't

catch any fish, but I tried my new outboard motor." Expressing unhappiness admits failure.

- Men offer advice. Advice taken shows that the advisor is smarter. In contrast, fixing another person's problem communicates subservient status.
- Men talk more in public. High status men talk the most. Men interrupt each other, to increase their talk time.
- Equal men prefer to talk sitting side-by-side, not looking at each other.[223] Driving is ideal for a conversation with a man. Men talk to each other face-to-face only within a hierarchy (e.g., a boss sitting at his desk), or in a confrontation.
- "Playful insults and teasing put-downs are a common way that men and boys show affection and intimacy."[224]

Women: "Rapport" Talk

Women communicate to establish egalitarian support circles:

- Supporting each other—"You're doing great!"
- Complimenting each other.
- Agreeing or saying "we're the same."
- Putting themselves down—"I'm not smart like you!"
- Making suggestions, especially to do things together—"Let's clean the house today"—instead of issuing orders.
- Asking for help, and offering help, to show rapport and equality.
- Instead of offering advice, women do the work themselves.
- Preferring intimacy to independence.
- Talking more in private.
- Gossiping or telling each other secrets, to demonstrate equality and intimacy.
- Women prefer to talk sitting face-to-face.[225] Women feel threatened when approached from behind.

Men Should Learn to Speak "Womanese"

Men have to learn two languages: "manese" to get to the top of the Great Male Hierarchy (and so attract women), and "womanese" to make a woman feel the equality, kindness, and support she's used to receiving from other women. Speaking "womanese" is the most important dating skill a man can learn.

The men at the top of the Great Male Hierarchy often have the worst relationships with women. Smart men devote years of higher education to learn "lawyerese" or "computerese." Then they spend one weekend in a John Gray seminar learning "womanese."

Instead, practice your "womanese" with every woman you meet. Make every woman feel good about herself. This includes old ladies, cleaning staff, and your sister-in-law.

Men with overdeveloped cerebral cortexes look down from their corner offices and wonder why women go for losers. The leader of a three-punk motorcycle gang, who plays guitar and knows the words women want to hear, scores all the women he wants. An MBA managing sixty employees can't get a date, if he only knows how to talk about business.

Men's Mistakes
- Interrupting—women's #1 complaint.
- When women talk about their problems, men give advice for fixing the problem. Women instead are asking for emotional connection.[226]
- Put-downs. Never tell a woman that she's ugly, stupid, short, or fat. Not even when you're joking.
- Don't argue, disagree, or correct facts. Listen for things a woman says that you can agree with, instead of listening for points to disagree about.
- Lecturing. Nothing is more boring to a woman than a man endlessly talking about his work or hobbies. Women smile, nod, and act interested, because this is how women listen. Men interpret this as encouragement to continue talking.[227]
- Lack of eye contact. Don't stare at a woman's breasts. Don't look at other women.
- Not listening. At least half of "good communication skills" is listening. (However, researchers have found that the commonly taught marital counseling technique of "active listening" doesn't improve relationships.)

Women's Mistakes

This list is shorter:

- Don't say "no" when you mean "yes" (page 67), or "yes" when you mean "no" (page 68).
- Women shouldn't speak "manese," e.g., "trash talk" after a game.

Don't try to compete with the guys; it won't impress anyone. Remember, one of the reasons they like you is because you don't offer yet more competition to the already existing male egos.[228]
— Chrissie Hynde's advice to aspiring female rock stars

Emotional Communication

Emotional messages hide in factual communications.[229]

Emotional messages can be verbal, e.g., inviting a woman to a party. Or emotional messages can be nonverbal, e.g., offering a man a place to sit.

Emotional messages can be positive (e.g., "I like you") or negative (e.g., "I don't like you"). Responses can be positive, negative, or ambiguous.

Good communicators respond to the emotional message as well as to the factual message. Good communicators respond positively to negative and ambiguous emotional messages.

Dating: Ambiguous Responses to Positive Emotions

In dating, the most common communication problem is ambiguous responses to positive emotional messages.

E.g., a man asks a woman out to a movie Friday night. His factual message is about the movie. His emotional message is, "I feel romantic attraction to you. Do you feel attraction to me?"

The woman responds, "No, I have other things to do Friday night." She's responding negatively to the factual message, and ambiguously to the emotional message. She's thinking, "You're probably a loser, but I'm not 100% sure, and the other men I'm dating are losers too, so keep asking me out. Maybe some night I'll be so desperate that I'll go out with you. God, I hope not."

The man responds, "What about seeing a hockey game Saturday night?" The woman again responds, "No, I have other plans Saturday night." They can go on for weeks without asking or answering the deeper message. Miscommunication wastes their time.

The woman could directly answer the emotional message. She could say, "I think you're attractive. Let's get together another time." Or, "I don't find you attractive and don't want to do anything else with you." It's hard to imagine that a woman would speak directly. You can see why we hide emotional messages in factual statements.

Or the man could clearly communicate his deeper message: "Do you feel attracted to me?" Again, it's hard to imagine a man directly asking an emotional question.

But clearly communicating emotional messages will improve your relationships. Try it. At first you'll say embarrassing things. With practice you'll master emotional communication.

Relationships: Respond Positively to Negative Emotions

In relationships, the most common communication problem is negative responses to emotional messages.

E.g., a couple agrees to meet at a restaurant. He's twenty minutes late. She points this out (a factual message) and her body language and vocal tone communicate that she's angry (an emotional message).

He responds negatively, "Only twenty minutes. What's the big deal? Last week you were thirty minutes late."

Negative, ignored, and ambiguous responses don't change your partner's negative emotions.

Successful couples respond positively to negative messages. E.g., he responds, "I'm late because my boss gave me a lot of work, but all day I was counting the minutes until we'd be together."

Playful Partnering

Relationship masters use humor to respond to negative emotions. The key word in that sentence was *masters*. Humor used badly will get you into deeper trouble.

Play a game (see page 16). E.g., you're twenty minutes late. Ask your partner to pretend to be angry. She looks at her watch, paces, and says, "He's one minute late. He doesn't love me. Now he's two minutes late. I should have married Fred the accountant. He was boring but punctual..."

You pretend to be somewhere else. You dreamily think aloud, "I love her cute little nose, I love her kissable lips....Oh no, look at the time, I'm late! She hates it when I'm late! I'd better stop and buy her flowers. No, that'll make me more late!"

Then you meet. She expresses anger, impersonating Jack Nicholson in *The Shining*. You express drippy, romance novel love. If she doesn't laugh, you get drippier, until she's laughing.

Now repeat the game, switching roles.

You acknowledge that you understand her emotional message, and switch your partner from negative to positive emotions.

Emotions Are Contagious

Consciously or unconsciously, people mimic each other's emotions. We *infect* each other with our emotions.[230] Your emotional state results primarily from the people around you, not from what you do or think.

If you can't get dates, maybe you're infecting people with negative emotions. No one wants to be infected with anger, distrust, anxiety, or low self-esteem. Instead, infect people with positive emotions.

Women's Dating Lies

> I felt a kind of pleasure in accepting at face value all the counterfeit currency she had passed off on me.[231]
> — Giacomo Casanova, 18th-century Italian lover

"No" Means "Yes"

40% of college women admitted that they'd said "no" when they meant "yes" to male sexual advances.[232]

Female rodents, ungulates (e.g., deer, elk, water buffalo),

canines, and primates solicit mating by alternately approaching and withdrawing from their selected male.[233]

Females use "approach-withdrawal" behavior to attract higher-status males. An "alpha" male gets many mating offers from females. Plus, he has to defend his territory against other males. He has to plan the next hunt or protect his harem from predators. A female has to make the male ignore the other stuff, and instead focus on her.

A high-status male will ignore a low-status female's approach, unless she looks easy. But if she appears to be too easy, her status drops even further, and he'll reject her. She has to play "hard to get" to increase her status. But this makes him drop the chase because she's no longer easy. She approaches again, repeating the cycle. If she skillfully plays the game, she increases his judgment of her status, and makes him focus on her, while paying less attention to other females. "Approach-withdrawal" behavior also avoids aggression from higher-ranking females.[234]

"Approach-withdrawal" behavior alternates masculine and feminine sexuality. A woman uses masculine sexuality to aggressively get a man's attention. She then switches gender roles to feminine sexuality and lets him chase her.

People endlessly debate whether treating a person badly makes him or her do what you want. Women tell their girlfriends to treat men badly. Men tell their buddies to treat women badly. Alternating interest and disinterest is "approach-withdrawal" behavior. It works, if played skillfully. But if you don't have the skills to play well, don't play these games.

"Yes" Means "No"

"Toxic niceness" is something most women are trained in from early childhood, and the most common manifestation of this malady is saying "yes" when you don't necessarily mean it. Which leads to doing things you don't really want to do. Which in turn leads to resentment, which tends to leak out in all manner of bizarre ways: snappish behavior, smashed dinnerware, prolonged periods of pouting...Being in touch with your inner bitch eliminates resentment because it frees you to say

"no"...Being in touch with your inner bitch does not mean that you indulge in poor behavior, such as hissy fits and manipulation...[rather, it means] using the handy catch-phrase "I don't think so."[235]
— Elizabeth Hilts, *The Inner Bitch Guide to Men, Relationships, Dating, Etc.* (1999)

When women talk to each other, they use inflection and body language to communicate, "I don't agree with you, but I'll accept your view because I value our relationship."

This communication style doesn't work when women talk to men. In the Great Male Hierarchy, passing a message down a chain of a command eliminates the emotional content. Organizations train men to hear literal messages, and ignore emotional subtext.

Men shouldn't "play games." E.g., a man may chase a woman while pretending to be "friends" (especially if he fears rejection). Women, in general, are better at dating and can lead men in circles if they try to "play games." Stay with clear, direct communication.

Jealousy

My guy and I have a loving relationship, but...I crave attention from other men. I flirt with every guy in the bar, including men my friends are after. I never take it any further than that, but I get off on making men swoon. Is there something wrong with me?[236]
— letter to *Cosmopolitan*

Women are twice as likely as men to intentionally cause jealousy.

Women cause jealousy to test the strength of the relationship, and to increase their partners' commitment. Jealousy increases sexual passion.[237] Jealous couples are more likely to marry. Revenge, bolstering self-esteem, and punishment aren't typical reasons for women to use jealousy.

Boyfriend Lies

25% of women living with men say they don't intend to marry their partners. Most explained that their partner's income or education was too low.[238]

These women wanted monogamous relationships, so they "hooked up" with a boyfriend. But they're not satisfied with their boyfriend, so they're keeping their eyes open for better prospects. If the boyfriend realizes this, he might cheat or end the relationship. Navigating through this dilemma sometimes requires lying:

- A man asks a woman's friend whether she has a boyfriend. "Yes," the friend replies, "but she wants to break up." He asks her out. She rejects him, saying that she has a boyfriend.
- A woman flirts with a man. When he asks her out, she says that she has a boyfriend.
- A woman accepts a lunch date with a man. After he pays the bill, she starts talking about her boyfriend.
- A woman refuses a date, saying that she recently broke up with a boyfriend and needs time to recover. Two weeks later she has a new boyfriend.

The message in all these examples is "I'm not 100% satisfied with my boyfriend so I checked you out, but you're not worth leaving my boyfriend for." He refuses to hear that he's inferior to another man. He instead accuses her of lying. (She may also be trying to make her boyfriend jealous.)

Men's Dating Lies

We have different rules for interactions between friends and strangers (see "Adult Friendship," page 84). Men's dating lies cross the boundary between friends and strangers.

A man may feel that he knows his object of desire, and so believe that they're friends. He may have watched her and overheard her conversations with her friends. Or, in this electronic age, he may have seen her on television or listened to her music and feels that he knows her. But as long as he's a stranger to her, he should interact with her according to the rules of strangers.

Or a man may think that acting like a friend will make a woman like and trust him. That works with equal partners. E.g., two men meet while fishing. If they're friendly to each other, they become friends (see "Equality," page 82). In contrast, imagine going into a bank to ask for a loan. There's nothing wrong with being friendly, but friendliness won't affect whether you get the loan. Dating is like applying for a loan. If a woman decides not to go out on a date with you, being friendly isn't going to change her mind.

Unsolicited Gifts

Friends give each other unsolicited gifts. Friends don't expect anything in return.

If you receive an unsolicited gift (e.g., a man finishes *People* magazine while eating lunch at a restaurant, and then gives it to the waitress), say that you don't want it but you know someone (e.g., a co-worker) who'd like it. If the giver backpedals and insists that the gift is only for you, don't accept it.

Solving a Problem

Friends help each other solve problems. But friends don't overplay minor problems into major problems. And friends don't cause problems, and then offer to fix them.

E.g., a man and woman arrive at a hardware store after it closes. He asks what she needs to buy, and she replies that she has a leaky faucet. It's OK for him to say that another store across town is open late. It's not OK for him to insist that she accompany him to the other store, and insist that she let him fix her leaky faucet.

Refusing to Hear "No"

Your best friend says that she doesn't want a birthday party this year. You ignore her "no," reserve the back room of her favorite restaurant, invite all of her friends, and decorate the room with banners and balloons. Your friend has a great time.

It's not OK for a stranger to refuse to hear "no." If a woman gives in to a minor allowance, e.g., carrying her groceries up to her apartment, she'll give in to bigger advances.

For more about recognizing predatory men's lies, read *The Gift of Fear*, by Gavin De Becker (1997).

LIFE STAGES

CHILDHOOD—SEEKING UNCONDITIONAL LOVE

Remember *Leave It To Beaver*? Every episode, Beaver Cleaver did something to get in trouble. E.g., he hit a baseball through a neighbor's window. No matter what trouble he got into, his parents loved him. The episode ended happily.

Children learn by making mistakes. They need an adult who'll fix the mistake, and then forgive them. Children need an adult who gives them unconditional love.

Adults who didn't receive unconditional love as a child spend the rest of their lives seeking a partner to give them that. Such individuals include physical abuse survivors, substance abusers, or individuals with mental illnesses.

When such individuals handle life poorly they test each new relationship. E.g., your new lover steals $50,000 from you, totals your car, then has drunken sex with a stranger and passes on a sexually transmitted disease to you. You might say, "That's OK, dear, I love you no matter what you do" (see page 206). More likely, you end the relationship and your ex-partner looks for a new lover.

Handled better, the individual seeks a brother or sister relationship. If you don't have a sibling, ask someone to be your brother or sister. Explain the relationship you want. And say what won't be in the relationship—e.g., borrowing money, loaning your car, or having sex. The Greeks called this *storge*, or the love of brothers, sisters, or comrades who have been through difficulties together.[239]

72

ADOLESCENCE—SEEKING ROMANTIC LOVE

First, starting at around age eleven, an idealistic image of life grows in intensity throughout the middle teens. Second, somewhere around age fourteen or fifteen a great expectation arises that "something tremendous is supposed to happen." Third, adolescents sense a secret, unique greatness in themselves that seeks expression. They gesture toward the heart when trying to express any of this, a significant clue to the whole affair.[240]
— Joseph Chilton Pearce, *Evolution's End* (1992)

Adolescent boys are easy to understand. They seek approval for accomplishments. They dream of winning the big game, playing guitar in a heavy metal band, and dating the prettiest girl in the school.

In folktales, adolescent boys go on quests for treasure. They overcome obstacles not by force of will but instead by listening to advice from seemingly unimportant creatures. In the end, they marry a princess.

Adolescent girls are harder to understand. On the surface they seem to care only about shopping, clothes, music, and movies—and talking about boys. Adolescent girls expend as much effort deciding what to approve as boys spend seeking approval. But what mental processes do girls use to approve something? (Contrary to popular belief, adolescent girls aren't sheep. They don't buy stuff solely because their peers bought it.)

In folktales, an old woman imprisons a young woman in a tower, castle, or kitchen (the old woman symbolizes the life stage the young woman is trying to grow out of—see page 206). There the young woman passively waits for Prince Charming to recognize her beauty and rescue her. This is a metaphor that women want men to see their inner beauty, that each young woman feels that something stops men from seeing her emerging true nature, and that women feel love when a man breaks through that barrier. When a man connects to a woman's inner self, she gives her approval. Similarly, women give their approval when clothes, music, or movies connect to their inner selves.

Adolescents give and receive conditional love—love for what makes an individual special.

Anima and *Animus*

Men are more-or-less unaware of their *anima*, or feminine aspects of their personalities. Women are more-or-less unaware of their *animus*, or masculine energy. When you meet a person of the opposite sex who embodies the hidden, contrasexual elements of your personality, you feel whole. You feel as if something's been missing all your life, and now you have it.

We feel passionate love (what the Greeks called *mania*) for these individuals. But we don't love the other person—we love ourselves, as reflected in the mirror of the other person.

Traditionally, men don't develop feminine skills (e.g., cooking) or feminine emotions (e.g., nurturing). A traditional man marries a woman who embodies these underdeveloped aspects of himself.

Conversely, a traditional woman doesn't develop a career, or use masculine emotions, e.g., assertiveness. She marries a man who'll do these things for her.

Together, a traditional couple can be one complete person, and enjoy a fulfilling relationship. A traditional relationship can enable a man to fully develop his masculine side, e.g., excel at his career. A woman can fully develop her feminine side, e.g., excel as a mother.

But each individual is unbalanced. For many people today, becoming a balanced, whole individual is as important as forming a supportive relationship. Such an individual uses passionate relationships to develop hidden personality elements. Then the individual no longer needs the relationship.

But, more often, we refuse to accept our hidden personality elements. Our partner reminds us of aspects of ourselves we don't want to be aware of. We feel both passionate love and hatred for our partner, and don't mature.

Psychologists say that the #1 complaint in marital counseling is that the "cute and quirky" qualities that attracted the partners to each other became annoying after the wedding. E.g., a shy but dependable man marries an outgoing, impulsive woman. He envies her ability to have fun. She admires his steady work ethic. But after they marry, she wants to go out in the evenings. He prefers to stay in. Compromising wasn't a problem when they dated a few nights a week, but now they have to compromise every night.

Ideally, he grows more like her, e.g., enjoying social dance classes. She grows more like him, e.g., taking night classes at a community college.

Projection

We sometimes recognize an element of ourselves in other individual. We then *project* additional personality elements onto the person. You imagine a future life together. You picture the beautiful home you'll share, the successful careers each will support in the other, and the perfect children you'll raise.

Each additional element gives reality one more opportunity to shatter your fantasy. Anything your object of desire says or does differently destroys your invented world. Eventually, everything your object of desire does hurts you, and you hate the person.

Archetypally, the imprisoned princess waits for her knight in shining armor. He'll solve all of her problems, and then they'll marry and live happily ever after. Young women project this ideal onto their lovers. But sooner or later, each woman sees reality. His armor is dented and has rust patches. His horse has a bad leg. Dragons defeat him more often than he defeats them. Her fantasy shatters. She's angry that he deceived her. He's stunned that one day she loved him, and the next day she hates him.

Alternatively, the knight rescues the princess—then rides away to find another dragon to fight and another princess to rescue (see "Becoming A Couple," page 139).

You used to stir my imagination. Now you don't even stir my curiosity. You simply produce no effect. I loved you

because you were marvelous, because you had genius and intellect, because you realized the dreams of great poets and gave shape and substance to the shadows of art. You have thrown it all away! You are shallow and stupid! My god, how mad I was to love you! What a fool I have been. You are nothing to me now. I will never see you again. I will never think of you. I will never mention your name. You don't know what you were to me, once. Oh, I can't bear to think of it. I wish I had never laid eyes upon you. You have spoiled the romance of my life.
— Oscar Wilde, *The Picture of Dorian Gray* (1890)

Teenage boys project their *anima* onto a girl. But the girl does things that aren't what he projected. The version in his head and the real girl conflict. This upsets him. He's happier loving her from a distance. If she likes him, she can't understand why he stops calling her when she starts paying attention to him. If she dislikes him, she finds it creepy that the boy has fantasies about her.

Adolescent *mania* is unrequited as often as it's mutual. Young men average three unrequited loves between 16 and 20. Young women average only 1.6 unrequited loves between 16 and 20.[241] I.e., teenage boys are less successful at love than teenage girls.

The switch between passionate love and passionate hatred isn't limited to teenagers, as anyone who's gone through a divorce can tell you.

Fear of Intimacy

Adolescents aren't capable of intimate relationships. They fall in love with projected images. Or they try to be someone else's projection. There's no intimacy because real people never connect.

Intimacy scares adolescents. Intimacy forces you to see parts of yourself that you wish you didn't have. Weakness, stupidity, sexual ignorance or inadequacy, and other faults come out in intimate relationships. Adolescents break off a relationship rather than experience their *shadow* aspects.

Young adults may think they're ready for an intimate relationship, but only with Mr. or Ms. Right:

So many people save loving. I call them "emotional virgins." Save really giving their heart away, surrendering, opening up, sharing, because they want to save it for the right person. The problem is when the right person comes along you don't know anything about loving.[242]
— Barbara De Angelis, *Coming Alive With Love* (1985)

"Emotional virgins" fear showing their inner selves to anyone who doesn't perfectly mirror their *anima* or *animus*. These individuals aren't ready to accept a real partner.

How To Make Your Object of Desire Want You

Instead of imagining your wonderful life with your object of desire, manifest your dream without the person. Ironically, this will make the other person more likely to want you.

E.g., a woman has a good job and a stable life. She's attracted to a jazz musician. His improvisations loft her emotions to heights she's never experienced. She wishes she could do that, but tells herself that she can't.

They date. She finds that he's underemployed and impoverished. Her first reaction is to offer the elements of her personality that she's aware and proud of. She tells him that if he marries her, he'll get health insurance. He isn't moved to propose.

He offers her the elements of his personality that he's aware and proud of. He asks her, on the spur of the moment, to accompany him to Jazz Fest in New Orleans. She can't take vacation time from work without six months planning.

She's right that what he *needs* is health insurance. More generally, he needs an opposite partner. But he *wants* a woman who's like himself—a woman who'll drive to New Orleans on the spur of the moment. He wants a woman who shares the aspects of himself that he's aware of and proud of.

The couple is right for each other, but their approach is wrong. She should identify why she's attracted to him, and develop those elements of herself. E.g., she's always wanted to develop her singing. She could ask him to give her voice lessons. He'll feel that she's becoming the type of woman he wants.

He could appreciate her ability to go to work every day. Instead of asking her to drive to Jazz Fest, he could ask her to manage his career. She'll feel that he's becoming the type of man she wants.

After she develops her singing she may no longer need him. After he's a financial success he may no longer need her. Or they may marry. Either way, they'll live happily ever after.

Identifying why you feel attracted to an individual is difficult. In contrast, explaining why your object of desire should want you is easy. Have a mutual friend ask each of you (separately) why each person should want the other. (Hint: ask a gay or lesbian friend, who understands both masculine and feminine thinking patterns.)

Developing an Adult Identity

The first crisis typically hits during our early 20s...We either don't know what we want to do with ourselves (start up a cyber-chic website? go to law school?) or can't seem to transform our idea of what we want to do into reality (how does one become a world-famous travel writer who journeys from one land of lush to another investigating such intriguing topics as orangutan rehabilitation in Bukit Lawang?). If we base our entire identity on vague or unobtainable plans due to lack of experience, we are ripe for crisis...

The second crisis usually hits during our mid to late 20s. After we've established a crude model of adulthood by which we've been living, we finally regain enough strength lost from our first crisis to acknowledge that the model we've created is not working. Various external influences typically propel the second identity crash: a friend gets a huge promotion...or the guy we thought we one day might marry goes on a three-day "vision quest" in the Rockies, comes back, and breaks up with us...or a friend gets pregnant, and due to pheromone influences beyond our control, we are overwrought by primal urges to get married and procreate, making us burst into tears at the mere thought of buying tiny baby socks.[243]
— Julia Bourland, *The Go-Girl Guide* (2000)

When I grow up I'll be stable...[244]
— Garbage, "When I Grow Up" (1998)

The primary work of adolescents and young adults is to develop adult identities. In high school, they make new friends. They try different sports or hobbies. In college, they consider different majors or careers. Maybe they try different sexual experiences. After college, they move to different neighborhoods or cities.

By 26, most individuals have a job, a relationship, and a community. They've created their first full adult identities. But they're unhappy with at least one aspect of their lives. E.g., an individual may have a good job, but is unhappy with her relationship. Or she may have the partner she wants to spend the rest of her life with, and a job she can't take another minute of.

Between 26 and 30, individuals change at least one aspect of their identities. If you want to marry a 26-year-old, be open to a career change or a move across the country. By 30, most individuals are comfortable with their identities and ready to settle down in a committed, long-term relationship.

Be wary of individuals who didn't go through identity crises as a young adult, e.g., a 30-year-old doctor who wanted to be a doctor since she was five. Individuals who don't have these identity crises when they're young have worse identity crises later in life, after they've made commitments to career, marriage, or children.

Too Little Adult Identity

Men and women emphasize their similarities to attract mates. Younger people, lacking strong identities, easily adapt themselves —sometimes by lying—to another person's likes and dislikes. Without a fully developed adult identity, everyone will love you, because whatever they are, you are too. Other people will easily project their ideals onto you.

Without an adult identity, you won't be able to say *no* to suggestions. You won't do unpleasant but necessary work. You can't hold down a job or work out problems in a relationship.

Too Much Adult Identity

Too strong an identity can make you unable to adapt to a changing world. An inflexible person can't learn and grow. Such a person can't adjust or subsume his or her identity to form a *dyad* as a couple (see "Dyad Trouble," page 150).

A strong, clear identity is difficult for others to project onto, so few people will feel adolescent *mania* for you.

Adjust your identity when you get something you want, e.g., a new job or relationship. Bringing your old identity into the new situation may get you into trouble. When a change is undesired, you're more "on guard" to look for ways that you'll need to change.

> **The most dangerous moment comes with victory.**[245]
> — Napoleon Bonaparte

Integrity

A well-chosen adult identity fits your personality and fits the world around you. An adult identity that doesn't fit your personality causes mental illness or depression. E.g., a man who is outgoing, fun-loving, and gregarious becomes depressed if he chooses a solitary career. A woman who enjoys quiet solitude develops anxiety disorders if she chooses to be a paramedic in a violent city.

An adult identity that doesn't fit the world around you causes separation from society, or *alienation*. If you choose a career for which there are no jobs (e.g., poet), or dress outlandishly or slovenly, or cultivate anti-social eccentricities (e.g., refusing to enter rooms with fluorescent lights), you won't receive material or social rewards. I.e., you'll be poor and lonely.

Integrity is the fusion of your public and personal selves. Whether you're a celebrity or a garbage collector, people will respect you if you have integrity. Buddhists call this "right livelihood."

Interpersonal vs. Inner Conflict

Traditional societies had fixed roles for farmers, blacksmiths, ministers, etc. (and for their wives and daughters). Our ancestors may have felt oppressed when faced with no choices, predictable futures, and pressure to conform. Identity crises caused interpersonal conflict. E.g., if the son of a tailor didn't want to be a tailor, he rebelled against his father.

Our society allows anyone to be anything. Parents no longer pressure their children into careers or arrange marriages. The world is changing so fast that following in your parents' footsteps no longer works—you'll likely change careers two or three times in your life. And whatever lifestyle you choose, you can find people who'll accept you, e.g., a lesbian triathlete stockbroker can move to San Francisco and find other lesbian triathlete stockbrokers.

Identity crises now produce inner conflicts, instead of interpersonal conflicts. Facing unlimited choices, uncertain futures, and minimal parental guidance, we have no one to rebel against but ourselves.

Adolescent Friendship

> Did you ever stop to think that a dog is the only animal that doesn't have to work for a living? A hen has to lay eggs, a cow has to give milk, and a canary has to sing. But a dog makes his living by giving nothing but love.[246]
> — Dale Carnegie, *How To Win Friends and Influence People* (1936)

Dogs give what the Greeks called *ludus*, or the enjoyment of each other's company.[247] Your dog enjoys being with you. You enjoy being with your dog. To win friends and influence people, be enjoyable to be with.

Your best friends are likely individuals you worked with or lived with. Choose a job where you'll work with people. Instead of living alone, share your home with several housemates.

The opposite of *ludus* is obligation. If you visit Aunt Millie only out of obligation, send her to a Dale Carnegie seminar.

Equality

Friendship requires equality. It's easy to be friends with individuals whom we're told are our equals, e.g., our college roommates. It's harder to be friends when we don't have equality thrust upon us.

To make friends with an individual more powerful than yourself, make it clear that you don't need the person's help. To be friends with an individual less powerful than yourself, make it clear that you won't help him or her.

A fast way to lose a friend is to act superior, or inferior.

Confusing Friends and Lovers

Sometimes a woman refers to the man she's having a sexual relationship with as her "friend." This communicates lack of commitment. She's either sleeping with more than one "friend," or she's dissatisfied with her "friend" and is looking for a better man (see "Boyfriend Lies," page 69). Either way, if your lover refers to you as a "friend," it's time to have an "our relationship" talk.

Don't have sex with your friends. This usually isn't a problem for heterosexuals, but for gays and lesbians it's a likely way to lose your friends. Friendships last longer than romantic love. Breaking off a love affair kills a friendship.

ADULTHOOD—FAMILIES AND FORGIVENESS

An adult sees his real partner, not a mirror reflecting himself. He sees his partner's faults, and loves her despite her shortcomings. The ancient Greeks called this love *pragma*. Psychologists call it *intimacy*. Christians call it *forgiveness*.

> The greatest happiness of life is the conviction that we are loved—loved for ourselves, or rather, loved in spite of ourselves.[248]
>
> — Victor Hugo

Adults give their partners space. E.g., on weekends he flies his glider. She goes to horse shows. They accept their differences. They lack the passion of 19-year-olds, but their relationship is stable.

When the knight becomes king and the princess becomes queen, their attention turns towards their kingdom. Adult partners focus not on each other, but on their family. If they don't have children, they may start a business together, or create art or music.

> Love does not consist in gazing at each other, but in looking together in the same direction.
> — Antoine de Saint-Exupery, author of *The Little Prince*
> (1943)

30s: Stuck Between Adolescence and Adulthood

Thirtysomething individuals can become stuck between adolescent *mania* and adult *pragma*. They're quick to see a potential partner's faults, and can't accept an imperfect partner. They want passionate love, but have outgrown the adolescent style of projecting ideals onto partners.

Such thirtysomethings reject partners who embody their hidden personality elements, and reject partners who don't. E.g., a man believes that "real men don't cry." Emotionally expressive women scare him, and he rejects them. Emotionally controlled women don't make him feel passion, so he also rejects them.

> By the time I got to 35, I had been disappointed enough times in a row that I was better at ruling men out than ruling them in.
> — Pam Houston, author of *A Little More About Me* (1999)

He swears off dating, because every relationship ends in disappointment. He'll accept only a perfect woman, in a passionate relationship. No woman meets his standards. He can see faults, but he can't accept faults. Our society encourages men stuck here to focus on career, sports, or hobbies.

Women stuck here expect that "Mr. Right" will magically appear, without the woman making any effort. Or the woman becomes a "man hater." Our society encourages women to blame men for their unhappiness.

Adult Friendship

Friendships determine success more than education or hard work.[249] Successful people have hundreds of friends. Friends connect us to new worlds of people. An individual with a wide variety of friends will accomplish more, with less effort, by asking the right person for help in any situation.

Adults create friendships by drawing boundaries. Boundaries draw people into parts of your life, as well as exclude them from other parts. Successful individuals quickly draw the right boundaries around new acquaintances.

Boundaries enable unequal adults to be friends (unlike unequal adolescents). E.g., a CEO and a janitor can be buddies on their company softball team—and return to their usual distance at work.

Rivals draw clear boundaries. Individuals can be rivals in one area, and friends in another.

The Internet is a boundary. It's easy to form friendships online, e.g., chatting on a discussion forum. Few on-line friendships become "real world" friendships. There's nothing wrong with that. On-line friends are another category, just as you have work friends, neighborhood friends, family friends, etc.

Companionate Marriages

In a companionate marriage, the couple shares careers, hobbies, friends, etc. Companionate couples also share parenting responsibilities.

Before 1970, companionate marriages were rare. In the past thirty years, this has become the most common type of marriage.

The problem with companionate marriages is boundaries. Each of us needs to be an individual, as well as to be part of a dyad (see "Dyad Trouble," page 150). In traditional marriages, the husband goes to work, the wife takes care of the home and the children, he goes to the Moose Club to see his friends, her friends come over for a coffee klatch, etc. The boundaries between individual and dyad are clearly drawn. But in companionate marriages, unclear boundaries can lead to one (or both) partners feeling a loss of individuality. In general, this makes the husband unhappy, if the couple is young, or the wife feels unhappy, if they're older (young men and older women value their independence).

Companionate couples should draw boundaries to spend some time apart. E.g., on weekends he flies his glider, and she goes to horse shows.

Your Village of Relationships

On my first visit home [to West Africa] after moving to the United States, I told my mother that just [my husband] and I lived in our house. To her, living like this was inconceivable; she thought I was crazy. It meant that we were getting no outside energy to support and strengthen our relationship. We were basically left with the impossible task of figuring things out on our own. In my own marriage, I now bring as many people as I can into the relationship....When you don't have a community of friends and family involved in a relationship, you base all your intimate expectations on your marriage. And that is too much to ask of any relationship. Of course, your partner is your friend and family, but to get everything from one person is impossible.[250]

— Sobonfu Somé, *The Spirit of Intimacy* (2000)

After more than a half-century of marriage, I can tell you that it is important to realize early on that no one person can give you everything that you want or need.[251]

— Old woman, quoted by Danielle Crittenden in *What Our Mothers Didn't Teach Us* (1999)

The ancient Greeks had six words for love:
- *Mania*, or adolescent passion (page 74).
- *Eros*, or sexual attraction (page 136).
- *Pragma*, or adult commitment and care giving (page 83).
- *Storge*, brotherly, sisterly, and comradely love (page 72).
- *Ludus*, friendship (page 81).
- *Agape*, the altruistic love of all creatures (page 86).

As we mature through each stage of our lives, we need—and give—different types of love. And each of us is more mature in some ways, and less mature in other ways. E.g., an individual may act maturely at work, but revert to adolescence when dating.

AGAPE—ALTRUISTIC LOVE

In 1993, 46-year-old former Wyoming cattle rancher, Grateful Dead lyricist, and founder of the Electronic Frontier Foundation John Perry Barlow fell in love with 28-year-old psychiatrist Cynthia Horner. A year later she died unexpectedly. In 1997, *This American Life* radio host Ira Glass interviewed Barlow:

> *Ira Glass:* Now that you've had this experience with her, do you find that you have this experience all the time in a smaller form, where you'll meet a group of strangers, and there'll be one whose eyes strike you, and you think OK, this person, I could see a part of this thing.

> *John Perry Barlow:* Absolutely. I feel an ability to attach on a moment-to-moment basis that is completely unlike anything that I felt prior to that. And I think it's a little disconcerting to other people because it's genuine on my side, and people are not used to having somebody just *dock* emotionally that instantaneously. I feel like I can see their souls, you know, their souls are visible to me.

In an adult relationship, you see your partner's good qualities, accept his or her faults, and emotionally connect. After you learn to do this with one person, you can connect with other people.

Traditionally, a man and woman who passionately love each other produce children, whom the parents passionately love. I.e., passionately loving one individual leads to passionately loving other individuals.

Religions teach individuals to feel passionate, non-sexual love for an abstract being, and then extend that love to other people. I.e., love for a deity helps them feel altruistic love for other people. The Greeks called this passionate, non-sexual, altruistic love *agape*.

RELATIONSHIPS

WHERE COUPLES MET

The #1 place people meet their spouses is "Other" (see Figure 3: Where Couples Met).[252] I.e., one-third of couples met in places where no other couples met. E.g., if you're an African explorer, you're more likely to meet your spouse while exploring Africa, and less likely to find your spouse in a Chicago singles bar.

School and work are the next-most common meeting locations (15–20%). Parties and bars are good for short-term (less than one month) sexual relationships (17–25%) and not bad for marriages (8-10%).

Churches are good for meeting marriage partners (8%), and poor for meeting short-term sex partners (1%). (This contradicts another dating advice book, which says that women in church singles clubs want sex "like bunnies."[253] This may apply only to certain churches. The book didn't specify where to find the best sects.)

Personal ads and singles cruises are poor places to meet anyone. Less than 1% of married couples met via a personal ad or on vacation.

To meet a relationship partner at work, work at an occupation with more opposite-sex co-workers. Organize social events outside work, e.g., company picnics or a co-ed softball team.

E.g., a male engineer works with other men. He signs up for community college evening classes in child development. The other child development students are women. After taking a few classes, he does a part-time internship at a daycare center. The other daycare workers are women. And he finds that many of the customers are divorced mothers. Plus he gets to build cool things with Legos.

E.g., a female daycare worker works with other women. She signs up at the community college for engineering classes. She enjoys drawing, and finds that she's good at drafting. Then she finds that draftspersons are paid twice what daycare workers earn.

To compare male and female percentages in over 200 occupations, see the *Statistical Abstract of the United States*, by the U.S. Department of Commerce (available in libraries or download free from http://www.census.gov/statab/www/). Look for the table "Employed Civilians, by Occupation, Sex, Race, and Hispanic Origin" (Table 593 in the 2001 edition). This table also provides racial statistics, if you want to meet, e.g., African-American men or Hispanic women. FYI, in 2000, engineering was 90.1% male and 90.6% white; child care providers were 97.7% female and 28.1% African-American or Hispanic.

To meet potential partners in school, take classes in which you interact with your classmates. Some business schools teach teamwork and leadership skills via group projects. Some progressive universities encourage instructors to   include

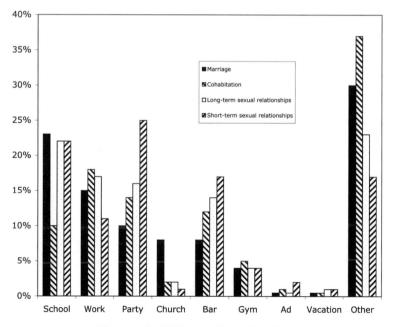

Figure 3: Where Couples Met

experiential segments (e.g., interactive games) in each class.

If you take an old-fashioned sit-in-a-lecture-then-write-a-paper course, organize a study group outside of class. If you're an older man, be a benevolent king. Don't try to "fit in" with the undergraduates. Show the students how to use the library (instead of the Discovery Channel). Coach them through oral presentations. Help them work as a team.

Who Introduced Couples

Friends are the primary introducers (35–40%) of couples of all types (see Figure 4: Who Introduced Couples).[254] The section "Adult Friendship" (page 84) shows how to increase your circle of friends.

Self-introductions are also important (32–47%). The researchers didn't specify whether successful relationships more often began when men introduced themselves to women, or vice versa.

Family members are good for helping you meet potential marriage partners (15%), but poor for helping you meet short-term sexual partners (3%). Take your mom to Festa Italiana or Irish Fest

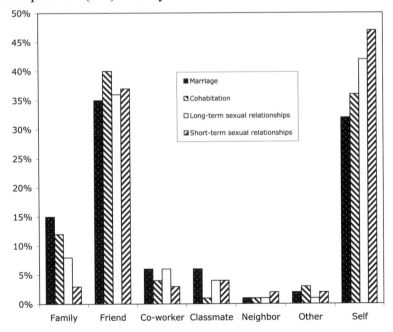

Figure 4: Who Introduced Couples

or Jewish Community Day. She'll find half a dozen mothers with children for you to meet.

Similarity and Dissimilarity

Couples are 70–90% similar regarding racial or ethnic group, education, age, and religion (see Figure 5: Similarity of Couples).[255]

But this *doesn't* mean that similarity attracts. Rather, race, education, age, and religion facilitate meeting. I.e., you're likely to meet individuals your age who go to your school and attend your church.

In the 1930s, most couples lived within *ten blocks* of each other when they met.[256] Improved transportation has widened our circles for meeting people, but we still tend to meet people who live in our neighborhoods. Because most neighborhoods aren't racially integrated, race is a surrogate for living in the same neighborhood (i.e., it would be interesting to study whether racially mixed neighborhoods produce more mixed-race couples).

Married couples are *dissimilar* in more ways than they're

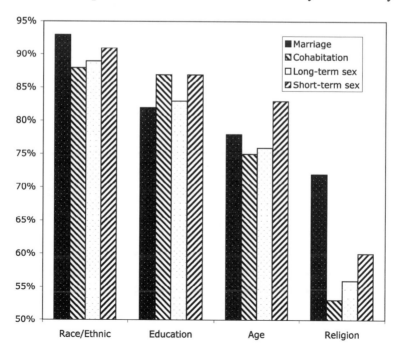

Figure 5: Similarity of Couples

similar, especially for factors that don't facilitate meeting. E.g., couples are, on average, dissimilar for personality types. Couples are also dissimilar for IQ tests, attitudes and opinions (e.g., whether mothers should work outside the home), hobbies and social activities, parents' economic class, physical and mental health, height, weight, hair color, eye color, physical attractiveness, exercise, vocabulary, day or night person, preferred foods, number of brothers and sisters, and birth order (some of these studies were conducted before 1970 and may be out of date, especially considering the post-1970 rise of companionate marriages, described on page 85).[257]

The section "Pheromones and MHC" (page 57) showed that similarity attracts for friendship, and opposites attract for sex.

Where to Meet Single Men and Women

Psychologists had seminary students write speeches on the topic of "The Good Samaritan." After finishing their speeches, each student was sent to another building to read the speech to an audience.

Between the buildings was an alley. In the alley was an actor pretending to be a disheveled man in need of assistance.

Half the students were told they were late and must hurry. These students ignored the man's pleas for help.

The other students were told they had plenty of time. These students stopped to help the man.

The psychologists concluded that simple changes in *context* powerfully alter individual behavior. In this and other experiments, psychologists have gotten individuals to do the opposite of their normal or professed behavior.[258]

Meeting Mr. or Ms. Right won't do you any good if he or she (or you) isn't thinking about romance. E.g., if you're in a hurry you'll walk right past Mr./Ms. Right, just as the seminary students walked past the man in need of help. Work on being in places where singles think about romance, when they're thinking about romance.

The Best Place to Meet Men

Men who take first aid classes are heroes. They're leaders. They care about other people.

To meet lifeguards, take the American Red Cross lifeguarding course. To meet Outward Bound instructors, take a Wilderness First Responder course. To meet firefighters, take an Emergency Medical Technician course.

The classes are stressful, so you get to know and respect each other. Plus the classes are "hands on" each other! And what you learn may save a life. Call your local Red Cross chapter or visit

http://www.redcross.org/

Another way to meet men is to select a club that sounds fun. All the things men do have organizations. E.g., you want to meet men who drive BMW motorcycles. Go to the BMW Motorcycle Owners Association website. E-mail your local club president, asking to be a passenger on the next ride.

The Best Place to Meet Women

Actresses are interesting, fun, unconventional—and beautiful. Meet them in acting classes or community theater.

Acting classes are scheduled playtime. You'll learn games to play with your nieces and nephews.

Acting classes improve your entertainment skills. You'll develop confidence in expressing emotions. You'll memorize poems (pick romantic ones). You'll discover that you can sing—and then women will show you what *swoon* means. Acting classes will make you more attractive to women.

Acting (and creative writing) classes show you each student's inner character. The gorgeous woman that you lusted after from day one will read a poem that makes you gag. The woman you didn't notice for the first three weeks will perform a scene that moves your heart.

Man Shortage or Woman Shortage?

In 1986, *Newsweek* reported that a single, college-educated 40-

year-old woman was more likely to be killed by a terrorist than to find a husband.

In 2001, the *Wall Street Journal* reported that men in their late 30s and early 40s will soon outnumber women five to ten years younger by two to one.[259]

Is there a "man shortage," as *Newsweek* reported? Or is there a "woman shortage," as the *Wall Street Journal* reported?

More boys are born than girls. But more boys and young men die. Around 25, men and women are equally numerous.[260]

Because women live longer than men, old women outnumber old men. And men tend to marry women two or three years younger. These factors cause a shortage of unmarried younger women, and a shortage of unmarried older men. But this effect is small (under 5%) until you're over 50 years old.

Birth rates vary over 40-year cycles (see Figure 6: Birth Rates, 1909-1998).[261] *Newsweek* and the *Wall Street Journal* reported opposite effects because their stories were 15 years apart.

The birth rate reached its lowest point in 1933. Prohibition ended that year. The birth rate reached its highest point in 1957. The birth control pill was introduced that year. The birth rate reached its next low point in 1973, and its next peak in 1990.

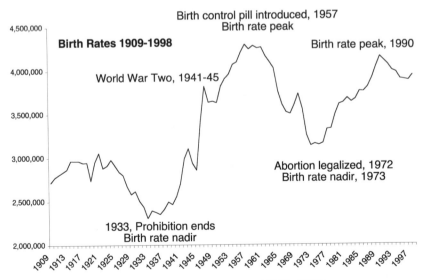

Figure 6: Birth Rates, 1909-1998

The lucky people are men born when the birth rate climbed (1933–1957, 1973–1990), and women born when the birth rate fell (1957–1973, 1990–1997).

Man Shortage or Commitment Shortage?

Men and women react differently to shortages of marriage partners.

During a "woman shortage," women are more likely to marry. During a "man shortage," women are less likely to marry, due to lack of quality partners.

During a "man shortage," men are less likely to marry, and more likely to "play the field" and have more relationships, with less commitment. During a "woman shortage," men are more likely to marry and stay married.[262]

I.e., during a "woman shortage" (e.g., of women born between 1957 and 1973), both men and women are more likely to marry. During a "man shortage" (e.g., of men born between 1933 and 1957), both men and women are less likely to marry. This partially explains the decreasing marriage rate between 1970 and 1990.

Create Your Own Man- or Woman-Advantage

Creating your own man- or woman-advantage may be easier than you expect. Young men and women selecting a university—or a major—can consider male/female ratios. Working men and women can change careers (see "Where Couples Met," page 88). Some one-industry small towns have lopsided male/female ratios. E.g., Vail, Colorado is rumored to have an eight-to-one male/female ratio among the young "ski bums" working at the resorts. Be warned, however, that Vail women say, "the odds are good, but the goods are odd."[263]

An older person can always create a man- or woman-advantage by dating individuals younger than him- or herself. Married people go "off the market," so single younger people always outnumber single older people, no matter your age or sex.

E.g., 25-to-29-year-old men who want to marry same-age women face five-to-four odds (1.22/1 ratio) against the men. But by dating 20-to-24-year-old women, the odds reverse and improve to three-to-four (1/1.3) in favor of the men.[264]

40-to-44-year-old unmarried men find equal numbers of unmarried women their age, and the same equality when dating women five years younger.

At age 45 and above, the advantage goes to men, whether they seek same-age or younger women. Unmarried men over 55 have a two-to-one advantage over women, both same-age and ten years younger.

FLIRTING

Female monkeys initiate more than 80% of matings.[265] In singles bars and at parties, women initiate two-thirds of flirting interactions.[266]

Women who follow *The Rules*—"men court, women choose"—and passively wait for men to court them get the 20% of men that other women don't want. I.e., they find that "the good ones are taken" by women who take an active role in courtship.

Instead, a woman should choose the man she wants to court her—i.e., "women choose, men court." E.g., the French romantic comedy *Amélie* charmed audiences with a young woman pursuing a young man—by making him pursue her.

Flirt with Everyone

Flirting is making a person feel good about himself. This usually means eye contact, smiling, compliments, and then making the person feel special.

Don't limit your flirting to attractive, single persons of the opposite sex. Try to make everyone you meet feel good about themselves. When you meet an attractive, single person of the opposite sex, you'll feel more confident. The rest of the time you'll make friends.

> Don't wait until you're in love to start loving in your life.
> Don't wait until you're in love to practice being attentive, to practice giving.[267]
> — Barbara De Angelis, *Coming Alive With Love* (1985)

Go out with a same-sex friend (e.g., a man goes out with a male friend). This makes it easier to flirt with two persons of the same sex (e.g., two women). After an interaction, discuss with your friend what you did right and wrong.

Peek-A-Boo

At a restaurant, catch the eye of a toddler. Then hide behind your menu. The kid will grin and excitedly play peek-a-boo with you.

Human brains are wired to play peek-a-boo. We love attention. Peek-a-boo is how we attract another person's attention.

Spy thrillers are full of peek-a-boo games. We love it when a mild-mannered character removes his disguise and reveals himself as James Bond.

Play peek-a-boo to meet singles. Make eye contact from a distance, and then look away. Hide behind something or someone. Repeat the eye contact-then-hide cycle for several minutes.

Women play peek-a-boo more subtly than men. If you're a man, don't get discouraged if your quarry seems to have only the slightest interest in you. If you're a woman, don't be too subtle. E.g., making eye contact via your compact's mirror won't register with most guys.

Tip Servers to Make an Introduction

Peek-a-boo reaches another level of subtlety when you involve a third person.

If you see two women or a group of women, or two men or a group of men, you can't approach and start talking to one individual. But some individuals can approach. In a restaurant, that individual is the waiter or waitress.

Write a note on your business card. Tip your server $20 to give your card to your object of desire. Your note should tell him or her to meet you in another room, out of sight of his or her companions, in five minutes.[268]

"Speed Dating"

You've got four minutes if you're lucky with Katie Couric on the *Today* show. When you minus out Katie's intro, Katie's outro, and Katie's verbose questions, you've maybe got two minutes forty-five seconds to get your point out. Research done at UCLA found that 93% of what an audience gets is non-verbal, and 7% is your words. It's what

lawyers call *demeanor*, it's what psychologists call *affect*, it's what actors call *attitude*.[269]
— Tom Alderman, Los Angeles media trainer

Nobody understands a damn word Deepak Chopra says, but it's who he's being that's just kind of mesmerizing.[270]
— Joel Roberts, KABC talk show host

A Los Angeles group has made dating like talk shows. In "speed dating," participants meet for seven minutes. Then a bell rings, and they move to the next numbered table. In 90 minutes, each participant gets seven speed dates. About 50% of participants get a real date afterwards.

"Speed dating" may sound harsh, but it's what everyone does. Communicating "the real you" in seven minutes or less isn't possible via verbal communication alone. Communicate via your clothes, body language, eyes, and voice.

Compliments

I was waiting in line to register a letter in the post office....while [the clerk] was weighing my envelope, I remarked with enthusiasm: "I certainly wish I had your head of hair."

He looked up, half-startled, his face beaming with smiles....

There is one all-important law of human conduct.... *Always make the other person feel important.*
— Dale Carnegie, *How To Win Friends and Influence People* (1936)

If you can be fearless, funny, and flattering, I'm yours.[271]
— Jane Ransom, *Playboy* (2000)

Compliments are a fundamental communication skill. Learning to give compliments will cost you nothing, and win you many friends.

Compliment Everyone
Like all skills, complimenting requires practice. Compliment

everyone, not just potential dates.

Begin with complimenting waiters and waitresses. If you say the wrong thing, leave a big tip.

Compliment old men, women pushing strollers in the park, the person behind you in the supermarket line, and your in-laws.

Compliment Smiles

Compliment the person's smile. Then smile. This will make the person smile.

The purpose of this compliment is to remind you to smile. You'll look more attractive when you smile.

Another purpose of this compliment is to make the other person smile. People feel happy when they smile.

Smiling is the second of Dale Carnegie's "Six Ways To Make People Like You."[272]

Compliment Eyes

Compliment the person's eyes. The purpose of this compliment is to remind you to make eye contact.

Look into the person's eyes long enough to mentally note his or her eye color.

If the person is wearing sunglasses, ask what color his or her eyes are. The person will then remove the sunglasses and you'll stare deeply into each other's eyes.

Compliment Names

Compliment the person's name. The purpose of this is the help you remember the person's name.

Associating the person's name with an interesting fact will help you remember his or her name. E.g., ask how his or her name is spelled (e.g., Rebecca vs. Rebekah), the ethnic origin, or the meaning of the name.

Ask if the person is related to a celebrity with the same last name. Read a history of your city or state to learn the names of local heroes and historical figures.

In a group, learn everyone's names. Whenever the group meets, greet each person by name. Introduce newcomers to each member. If remembering names is difficult for you, think of it as a brain exercise to prevent Alzheimer's (and use this as an apology when you forget someone's name for the 6th time).

Saying a person's name is the third of Dale Carnegie's "Six Ways To Make People Like You."[273]

Compare the Person to a Celebrity

When you compare a person to a celebrity, make sure the celebrity is physically attractive, and the right age. Don't tell a woman that she reminds you of Ally McBeal, or tell a man under sixty that he reminds you of Sean Connery.

Avoid Competitive Compliments

Avoid compliments about things you're competing on. Avoid compliments that put yourself down.

E.g., you lose a tennis game. Don't say, "Your serve is strong! I could never serve as well as you." This looks like a compliment, but is really a competitive comparison. You put the person in a difficult position. If he politely insists that your serve is good, he's impolitely rejecting your compliment. If he politely accepts your compliment, he's impolitely agreeing that you'll never serve well.

Such a compliment creates a hierarchy, not an egalitarian relationship.

Instead, make compliments when you're not in a competitive situation, or about something that isn't a competitive issue.

The Best, Most Difficult Compliment

Compliment what embarrasses the person.

E.g., if a well-dressed woman is driving a beat-up old car, say that she looks like a woman that blues musicians write songs about. Then improvise a blues song about her beautiful looks and her clunker car.

This increases the person's emotional range. The person feels embarrassment when you point out a fault. Then he or she feels good when you say that the fault is attractive.

Reflect Ordinary People's Extraordinary Lives
> You can make more friends in two months by becoming genuinely interested in other people than you can in two years by trying to get other people interested in you.[274]
> — Dale Carnegie, *How To Win Friends and Influence People* (1936)

Two of Carnegie's "Six Ways To Make People Like You" are *smiling* and *saying people's names*. The other four principles are:

- Become genuinely interested in other people.
- Be a good listener. Encourage others to talk about themselves.
- Talk in terms of the other person's interests.
- Make the other person feel important.[275]
> — Dale Carnegie, *How To Win Friends and Influence People* (1936)

These four principles can be rephrased, "Listen for extraordinary things people have done, then reflect this back to them."

Read books by Studs Terkel or Tom Wolfe. Listen to *This American Life* on public radio (or via http://www.thislife.org/). These journalists report the extraordinary lives of ordinary people.

Imagine that you're a reporter. Get people to talk about the extraordinary things they've done. This is a listening skill, not a talking skill, and is harder than it sounds. Everyone thinks that their lives are ordinary. E.g., a man who flies jet fighters thinks of himself as an ordinary fighter pilot.

Transition Points

People are open to new relationships when they're at transition points. Transition points include:
- Starting college.
- Moving to a new city.
- Starting a new job.
- Moving to a new apartment.
- Buying a new car.

Getting out of prison is a transition point. I live across the street from a corrections halfway house, full of beautiful young felonious women. I've resisted the temptation to go over and casually ask, "So, when do you get out?"

Transition points make people less critical of each other. E.g., a woman has graduated from college, found a good job, rented a cool apartment, and bought her first new car! In six months she'll be bored with the job, hate the cockroaches, and her Hyundai will leak oil. But now everything is big and new and wonderful. She feels that she's "on a roll." If a man walks into her life, she'll think he's another great part of her new life.

In contrast, a 34-year-old divorcée with two children, a house she's lived in for six years, a car she's driven for eight years, and a job she's had for ten years will be harder to date. Dating disrupts her routine. The annoyance of the disruption overrules the possible enjoyment of a new romance.

To meet new people, create a transition point in your life.

Dancing for Dummies

I have a friend who's a professional dancer. Women are in seventh heaven dancing with him. He leads so well that women who've never waltzed, hustled, or hip hopped are spinning around the dance floor. This is stereotyped gender role attraction at its best. He's in the driver's seat, she's in the passenger seat, and the ride is fun.

But I can't stand dance lessons. Most of the time I'm learning steps, i.e., dancing solo. When I dance with a partner I have to concentrate on the steps, not on connecting with my partner. If I connect with my partner, I forget the steps. This annoys her. Dance lessons make me look and feel stupid, and make me disconnect from my partner.

Women, in general, are better dancers and learn dances faster. Yet women expect men to lead them. This makes no sense until you consider the Great Male Hierarchy hardwired into our brains. Skilled dancers, and the women they danced with, created social dances. Social dances are intentionally difficult, so that women can easily separate the "alpha" males from the village idiots.

Men fantasize about winning the Superbowl, playing against other men. Women fantasize about winning dance competitions, led by a skilled, handsome, and romantic man (e.g., *Dirty Dancing*).

Try dance lessons. If you easily learn the steps and have fun, go for it. But if you're like me, focus on *connecting with your partner*. Make eye contact. Then *mirror* your partner's movements. Mothers and infants do this. It's how toddlers play peek-a-boo. It's hardwired into your brain. Mirroring makes two people emotionally connect.

At first, give your partner room. Don't touch her. As you intuitively connect, the two of you will find moves that you enjoy. Dance closer, touch, and lead. Now you're ready to ask a dance instructor to teach you spins and swings. Over time, you'll become a skilled dancer. But, unlike dance lessons, the journey will bring you and your partner together.

Making a Date

Ask for a date directly. Don't ask vague or indirect questions. Playing games invites the person to lie or play games.

Don't accept a vague or indirect answer. E.g., you're looking forward to an event. You ask a person out. The person says "maybe," meaning "no." You hear "maybe," meaning yes. Two weeks later, you figure out that "maybe" meant "no." But now it's too late to ask anyone else out. If a person says "maybe," or doesn't return your call or e-mail, assume that the person means "no." Ask someone else out.

If the person says "no," thank him or her for the clear answer.

Telephone Numbers
Ask for a telephone number or e-mail address.

A man should offer his card, but shouldn't expect a woman to call. A man should never give a work or voicemail number. This suggests that he's married and trying to trick her.

A woman concerned about her privacy or safety should rent a voicemail box, or give out her e-mail address.

Business Cards

A man's business card should communicate status. He should ask his supervisor to give him a more impressive job title. Or add a title given by a professional association. Or hire a graphic designer to create a beautiful card.

A man should write his home telephone number on his business card when giving it to a woman. He should add his home address so she can drive by and see what his house looks like.

E-mail Addresses and Personal Websites

Use an e-mail address that identifies your gender and age, e.g., "Ernie1959." Build a personal website with information about yourself, your photo, etc. Put the URL in your e-mail signature. Your e-mail recipients can then read more about you.

Excuses to Ask Personal Info

Take advantage of excuses to ask people about themselves. E.g., in a business class it's appropriate to "network" with classmates: "And where does your husband work? Oh, you're not married?"

How to Call

If a woman gives a man her telephone number, he should call her the next day.

He shouldn't wait two days. If he hesitates, she'll feel hurt and rejected.

If you get her answering machine, read a romantic poem (e.g., a Shakespeare sonnet). Women love romantic poetry.

Dress for Sex

Men's Clothes

Dress to communicate your gender. Masculine clothes have heavier fabrics. Colors are darker. Masculine clothes emphasize broad shoulders (e.g., epaulets), flat stomach (e.g., men's shirts tuck into their pants), slim waist and hips, and muscled legs.

Boring, conservative clothes are masculine. Creative, attention-grabbing clothes are feminine. To attract women, wear normal clothes. Grey with a designer label is good. Don't wear leather pants. Women assume that men who dress creatively are gay or mentally ill.[276]

A beard hides your face. Religious patriarchs and department store Santa Clauses are playing a role and want you to see the mask, not the individual behind the mask. In contrast, businessmen and politicians don't wear beards because hiding their faces makes them appear less trustworthy.

A full mustache communicates masculinity, dominance, and power. Its popularity varies between times and cultures—if you're not Hispanic, gay, or living in the 1970s, consider shaving.

Women's Clothes

Women's clothes draw attention to their breasts, waist, and hips. Depending on whether adolescence or maturity is in fashion, women's clothes either emphasize a flat stomach and thin legs, or make strong, sweeping curves to suggest fertility. Feminine clothes have lighter fabrics and brighter colors.

Play peek-a-boo to get men's attention. Intentionally tear your jeans or sweaters, show a little cleavage, or wear a slit skirt. Sexy materials—leather, latex, spandex—play peek-a-boo by suggesting skin without showing skin.

Wear an accelerator and a brake. A pink t-shirt displaying "Playmate of the Year" in glittering letters is like a car with an accelerator but no brake. Men won't hear "no." Instead, wear a conservative skirt with sexy boots, or vice versa.

Women shouldn't wear "trend of the minute" clothes. You'll impress the people who read women's fashion magazines—other women. Instead, wear "timeless" styles. Natural colors, patterns, and fabrics are timeless. Things not found in nature aren't.

The Best Pick-Up Line

The best conversation-starter is to interpret how a woman's clothes express her personality. Read *The Language of Clothes*, by Alison Lurie (2000), to interpret the colors, patterns, and styles of women's and men's clothes.

Then read *Big Hair: A Journey into the Transformation of Self*, by Grant McCracken (1996), to talk about her hairstyle. The chapter about blondes is worth the price of the book.

Dream Houses, Dream Relationships

Clothes are about flirting. Houses are about relationships. When you imagine your dream home, you also imagine your dream relationship. Creating your dream home may lead to your dream relationship. Conversely, living in a place that makes you unhappy will prevent you from forming happy relationships.

The most common home problem is commitment to the past, a.k.a. clutter. Clutter defines the old you. Donate your ex-self to Goodwill. Create space in your home for something new.

E.g., a woman's home was dominated by her ex-husband's piano. She couldn't start relationships. When she got rid of the piano she immediately found a relationship.[277]

If you're a man, communicate that you're relationship material:

- Display pictures of your family—especially of you playing with your nieces and nephews.
- Green, healthy plants communicate that you're capable of taking care of something.
- To make your living room communicate your personality, start by getting rid of the television. This will also give you time for a new relationship—Americans average four hours of television a day.
- A bed against a wall communicates that you intend to stay single. Create walking space on both sides of the bed.
- Women like clean bathrooms. Their sense of smell is better than men's. If you're incapable of keeping your house clean, just clean the bathroom. John Gray's next book will be *Mars*

and Venus in the Bathroom.

- Pizza, chips, and beer communicate "bachelor." Fresh fruits show that you buy groceries more than once a month. Diet soft drinks, exotic coffees and teas, and low-fat ice cream show that you understand women.

In *House as a Mirror of Self: Exploring the Deeper Meaning of Home,* by Clare Cooper Marcus and James Yandell (1995), the chapter "Becoming Partners: Power Struggles in Making a Home Together" shows how homes cause or solve relationship problems.

HOW TO WRITE A PERSONAL AD

REVENGE OF THE NERDS
Thick glasses, HP calculator, SAT 99th percentile, knows pi
to 16 digits. Great job, big house, pool. Better-looking than
Bill Gates.

I ran "Revenge of the Nerds" without the swimming pool, and got
one response. With the pool I got fifteen responses. Now I know
what women want.

I made a mistake running the following personal ad:

HIGH-TECH REDNECK
Million-dollar Los Gatos home with junk cars in yard. Italian
suits, cowboy boots. Likes country music.

I'd thought that country songs were made up. I thought that the
women in the songs weren't real. Then they all called me.

I wrote this personal ad for two dogs that needed a home:

TWO GIRLS...
One blonde, other brunette. Fun-loving. Enjoy long walks
on the beach, convertible cars, and heavy petting. Loyal,
good listeners. Both have four paws and adorable floppy
ears.

An alternative newspaper rejected the following personal ad:

FUN GOTH GUY
Look: tall, thin, pale, black leather. Attitude: dominance. Music: The Damned, Killing Joke, Bach organ fugues. Hobbies:
collecting memorabilia from serial killers, laughing mania-
cally in inappropriate circumstances, putting the "fun" back
into "funeral." Can I bite your neck on the first date?

This will date me, but I remember when alternative newspapers
didn't have decency standards.

Making Personal Ads Work

Less than 1% of married couples met via personal ads (see "Where Couples Met," page 88). Only 2% of short-term sexual relationships started with a personal ad. Less than one in 500 online personal ad users finds a partner. 23% haven't gotten a date in over a year.[278]

Personal ads are, in general, a poor way to find a mate. This is partly because most people write poor ads, and then place them in the wrong venues. The right ad in the right venue can work.

Write an Effective Personal Ad

Write your personal ad around *conversation starters*. E.g., writing that you're new in town prompts a variety of questions, such as "Where did you move from?"

In contrast, writing "I love sitting by a fireplace, talking about everything and nothing," prompts no responses.

Imagine that an individual approaches you at a party. Write out a conversation about yourself that fascinates this person. Now condense your responses into two or three sentences.

Imagine saying each sentence to a stranger. What would the person say in response? If you can't imagine a meaningful response, take out the sentence.

Now highlight every bragging point. Add self-deprecating humor. E.g., one of my ads said that I lived in a million-dollar home. I then added "with junk cars in the yard."

Run your ad through your word processor's spelling checker. Then run it through a grammar checker (in Microsoft Word, the grammar checker is under "Tools"). Now look in your Yellow Pages under "Editorial Services." Pay a professional editor $25 to edit your personal ad. Spelling and grammar errors make you look lazy and stupid. A polished, professional-sounding ad makes you look thirty IQ points smarter.

If you're in a big city, especially in the north or west, describe your looks and your money in your personal ad. In small cities, especially in the southeast, emphasize emotions and hobbies.[279]

Select the Right Venue

A magazine writer had less-than-great experiences with several big online dating websites. Then he won an eBay auction and paid $550 for a personal ad on a hip New York online women's 'zine. The magazine didn't usually have personal ads (i.e., his ad was a special feature). The result was 60 e-mails and "lots of" dates with interesting women.[280]

Buy an ad in each of the following venues:

1) Big online dating services, e.g., Matchmaker.com, Match.com, Kiss.com, AmericanSingles.com, or a big local newspaper. Buy a month's membership. If you don't get dates within a month, cancel your membership and try another website.

2) Specialized online dating services, e.g., BlackSingles.com, ChristianSingles.com, Salon.com, etc., or a specialized magazine or newspaper.

3) A website or publication that doesn't have personal ads, but attracts the type of person you want to meet (most couples met in "Other," see page 88). E.g., if you want to meet men who drive BMW motorcycles, go to the BMW Motorcycle Owners Association website. Ask, beg, and offer a large pile of cash to the website to run your personal ad as a special feature. Suggest that the website run two personal ads (one man, one woman) on Valentine's Day, that they auction the ads on eBay, and that they use the "event" for promotional publicity.

Feedback Ratings

Select an online dating service that has feedback ratings. The only one I know of is http://www.GreatBoyfriends.com/.

On eBay, buyers and sellers leave each other positive, neutral, or negative feedbacks. When you get ten positive feedbacks, eBay puts a gold star next to your name. Buyers and sellers know at a glance that you're trustworthy. If they want to be sure, they can read each comment written about you.

If personal ad websites had feedback, you could select only

individuals with a gold star. Then you could skip the ads and go straight to the reviews.

Other personal ad websites have surreptitious e-mail newsletters reviewing dates. These newsletters are only shared by women, and say only bad things about men.[281] This fosters a negative environment.

Checkboxes and Ideal Partners

> I've had some pretty funny experiences with married couples. For the most part they don't match well at all. At one event this woman was berating her husband for having answered the questions wrong. He said, "Yes, dear, yes, dear."[282]
> — Michelle McDonald, inventor of the "Matchstick" electronic device which lights up when you're near someone with similar interests

Since the 1960s, computer programmers have tried to find questions that instantly match an individual with his or her perfect mate. This might work for finding friends, but we're hardwired for sexual attraction to our opposites (see "Pheromones and MHC," page 57; and "Similarity and Dissimilarity," page 91).

> Your computer was right. Mitzi and I like all the same things: same food, opera, bike-riding, dogs. There was only one thing we didn't like—each other.[283]
> — Bernard Murstein, *Paths to Marriage* (1986)

The endless checkboxes on personal ad websites are worthless. We feel passion for individuals who reflect hidden elements of our personalities (see "Adolescent Relationships—Anima and Animus," page 72). You can't describe such a partner, because you can't see the hidden parts of yourself.

Listing intolerable qualities is also useless. E.g., lying is intolerable to you. Ask 100 potential mates whether they lie. Everyone will say that they never lie. Or smoking is intolerable to you. You might reject an individual who wants to quit, but needs a supportive partner.

A better way to describe your ideal partner is to list your favorite celebrities and why you like them.

Photos

Always provide a photo. Not providing a photo won't make people think that you have a beautiful mind.

Spend the money for a professional portrait.

Provide additional photos in different environments. E.g., if the first photo is a studio portrait, provide a second photo playing sports or playing with your nieces and nephews. Provide a full-body photo as well as a head shot.

Lastly, correct the brightness, contrast, and color balance. If you don't know how to do this, pay a camera dealer or Kinko's to prepare high-quality digital files.

Responding to Personal Ads

Women should respond to men's ads. If you wait for men to contact you, you'll only hear from the men that no other women want (see "Flirting," page 97).

A man should place his personal ad in many websites and publications, until he finds a venue in which women contact him.

When responding to an online personal ad, copy your profile and photo into your message. Don't expect the recipient to go to the website and look up your profile.

The Future of Personal Ads

Location-Based Cellphones

The newest cellphones have Global Positioning System (GPS) transponders. These cellphones can tell a 911 operator where you are, within a few feet. In a few years, when you join a singles club your cellphone will alert you when you're near another club member.[284] Your cellphone screen will provide the other person's profile—and send your profile to him or her. If you want to meet each other, your cellphones will guide you to each other.

On your home computer you'll select parameters—age, hobbies, etc.—and see a map highlighting where these people are now. E.g., you want to meet older men who enjoy cooking. On Saturday morning your computer may show that they're at the farmer's market, picking out ripe tomatoes.

Reverse Personal Ads

You'll see a list of local events. You'll check off events you'd like to attend. Then you'll search for other members who want to attend an event.

E.g., you click on Blues Traveler at the Paramount Theater. You then see all the single men or women who are going to the Blues Traveler concert. Because you both want to attend the event, you're guaranteed a date.

Road Trips

You and other singles fly to a new city each month. Single natives of that city have a weekend of group dates planned. You'll see the sights of a new city, and meet new people.

One weekend a month, you and singles in your city host a group of singles flying to your city.

Flying Affinity Class

Where are strangers intimately close for far too long? Prisons and Landmark seminars, yes, but these may not be people you want to meet. Instead, fly!

The *Wall Street Journal* suggests flying first class to meet the best potential mates.[285]

Airlines should sell *affinity class* seats. You'd fill out a form listing education, hobbies, marital status, etc. Then you'd select the affinity class passenger you want to sit next to. A good conversation is better than an in-flight movie.

♥

DATING

My best friend and I took two women canoeing. That summer was the worst drought in the state's history. The river was a little creek. We walked down the creek, looking at the crayfish and the minnows, pulling the canoe after us.

My friend and I wore heavy sneakers. The women wore sandals. His date got leeches between her toes. I removed them with my pocketknife. My date stepped on a rusty nail, where a farmer ran his cattle in the river. She later had to get painful tetanus shots.

Then we crossed a series of beaver dams. The beaver ponds were quagmires of mud and manure and flies. We wrestled the 17-foot aluminum canoe over each one. We got back to the car hours after dark, eaten alive by mosquitoes.

We got to know each other. We saw each other under stress. The women saw us solving problems. They saw our concern for their well-being. They saw us using muscle and determination.

My friend and his date were engaged less than a year later. My date and I were together on and off for eight years. Was it a good date or a bad date? If I'd known that there wasn't water in the river, I would've planned a different date. But the results of the date couldn't have been better.

On a date, take her outside of her normal realm.[286]
— Ron Louis, *SEXpectations* (1997)

Emotional Range

"Emotional intelligence" isn't about controlling your emotions. It's not about substituting positive emotions for negative emotions. It's about experiencing a full range of emotions.[287]

Civilization reduces the range of emotions you feel. In the civilized world, you never feel desperately thirsty or terrified of wild animals or hopelessly lost. But desperation resolved becomes joy. You can't feel the highest highs if you don't feel the deepest lows. The ideal date makes your partner—and you—feel a range of emotions.[288]

Dinner-and-a-movie doesn't facilitate a range of emotions. Instead, if you're both sports fans, go to a game. Hope that your team has difficult moments, but ultimately triumphs. The ideal date is an emotional roller coaster.

Outdoor sports—skiing, hiking, rock climbing—produce a wide range of emotions. Or take your date to a hot blues club in a dangerous neighborhood. But prepare for possible dangers. Before the date, drive to the club in the daytime. Find a safe parking lot nearby. Remember how to get back to the freeway.

What to Do on a Date

Personal safety is women's priority on dates with strangers. Don't talk about violent crime, guns, terrorism, etc. Meet in a public place in a safe neighborhood. Don't suggest hiking in a remote area. If the woman has a child, don't suggest bringing the child.

The ideal first date is breakfast at a large restaurant. This is safe and requires no planning. If it's a workday, you're already dressed nicely. If you're not interested in each other, you've lost only $15 and 45 minutes.

Don't talk about the weather, television, or work. You have only 45 minutes, so go straight to emotional connection. Ask what she's looking for in a partner. Or ask, "Women say that 'chemistry' is the most important thing in a relationship. What does 'chemistry' mean to you?"

Group Dates

The second date should be a group date. Women like group dates. Men can trade off leadership roles, putting less pressure on each man.

When the group is together, direct your conversation to a person of the opposite sex. But also include short periods of time when the men go off as a group, leaving the women together.

Play the Life Stories game. Each person has five minutes to tell her life story. Then she answers questions for five minutes. This game sounds simple, but the experience is profound. You'll be stunned at what you learn about people.

The Best Date a Man Can Take a Woman On

Lead a group date that shows off your entertainment skills. E.g., practice *a cappella* singing classic rock songs with two or three of your buddies. Go to coffeehouse "open mike" nights. Each of you asks a woman to watch your group perform.

Organize a group to write a humorous April Fools newsletter for your company or club.

Organize a group of friends to read a screenplay aloud. To make it more fun, have the men read the women's roles and the women read the men's roles. Find screenplays at

http://www.script-o-rama.com

The Best Date a Woman Can Take a Man On

Volunteer with a non-profit organization. When a man asks you out, suggest that he join you.

This tests both his commitment to you (see "Beautiful Young Women Don't Have It Easy," page 26), and his relationship skills. E.g., volunteer with Habitat For Humanity to see if he's a good worker, and gets along in a group. Volunteer with a homeless shelter to see if he can make lower-status individuals feel good about themselves (i.e., if he has ego problems). Volunteer with the Humane Society to see how he interacts with animals. Volunteer with children to see if he has good parenting skills.

Ending the Date

Ending the date first communicates that you're in control. Leave cash on the table to pay the bill, and walk her out to her car.

If you're a man, ask for a kiss. This will communicate to you whether she enjoyed the date, and if she wants to see you again.

If you ask whether she enjoyed the date, or if she wants to see

you again, she'll always say "yes" (see ""Yes" Means "No"," page
68). If you ask for a kiss and she says "no," she doesn't like you
and you won't get a second date.

If she "freaks out" when you ask for a kiss, say that it's
appropriate for her to thank you for asking, instead of grabbing.

Keep in mind that this is not a kiss for pleasure. A goodbye kiss
is quick. Keep your tongue in your mouth. You might kiss her
cheek instead of her mouth. A goodbye kiss is *one* kiss—not a
series. Stroke her hair, not her body.

If she asks for a hug instead of a kiss, again keep it brief.

If she offers to shake hands instead, it'd be romantic to bow and
kiss her hand—but practice this first!

Alcohol

Alcohol consumption is the strongest predictor of sexual intimacy
on first dates.

On first dates without drinking, college students usually hold
hands or have a casual kiss goodnight.

On first dates in which the combined drinking totals ten drinks
or less, couples usually neck (prolonged kissing with close hugging)
and may pet (touching the woman's breasts lightly through her
clothes).

On first dates in which the couple's combined drinking totals
more than ten drinks, the man usually fondles and kisses the
woman's breasts. Sexual intercourse isn't unusual on first dates
with heavy drinking.[289]

Alcohol consumption during dating negatively correlates with
the quality of the ensuing relationship.[290] I.e., if you want casual
sex without a relationship, drink on dates. If you want a quality
relationship without casual sex, don't drink on dates.

12 Dating Mistakes Men Make

Talking About Yourself
Women dislike men who talk only about themselves. Instead of

talking about how great you are, talk to make your date feel great about herself.

> Going to dinner and having nothing in common but work ...entire conversation was about work or him...it didn't seem to matter what I wanted to do or what I had to say...

Talking About Facts

Don't be a know-it-all. After 14.5 years of higher education, I know enough facts to fill a factotum. And when I convey those facts to women, they say, "I'm afraid I don't have a romantic interest in our acquaintance."

Narcissism

> He talked only about himself. He told me he had written a book about formerly married people. This formerly married person told me about his former marriage, about his life history, about his other books for general consumption, which all seemed to parallel his personal social and emotional history, and his other accomplishments. There wasn't a single question, and he clearly felt I should be incredibly impressed.
>
> His whole attitude was that I was very, very, very lucky to have this great expert on positive social interactions paying attention to me, a young free-lance writer....
>
> Finally, at about three, I said I had to go to another appointment. He was suddenly put off. He couldn't believe that a woman would leave first....He had to make the first move toward the exit. The feeling was so vivid, it was as if his beam of human energy abruptly shut off....
>
> Later on [it was] revealed that he...had been sleeping with his clients; he had kept a whole filing cabinet full of files on other women he'd had affairs with.[291]
>
> — Gloria Steinem

Never date a man who writes relationship books!

Narcissus was a beautiful young man. After a tiring day of hunting, he came to a clear spring. He kneeled to drink. He saw his reflection in the water. He thought that it was a beautiful water-spirit living in the spring. He fell in love with his reflection. He tried to kiss and embrace it. It fled at his touch. But soon it returned. He couldn't tear himself away. He lost all thought of food or rest while he gazed at his reflection. When he died, the gods created a purple and white flower, and named it after Narcissus.[292]

Compare Gloria Steinem's date to Narcissus. The psychologist talked and talked, hoping to see his brilliance reflected in Steinem's awe. He had no interest in Steinem, other than for her to act like a living mirror. As long as Steinem sat still and reflected him, he felt attraction to her. But when Steinem stood to leave, she was like the rippling water of Narcissus's pool. He no longer saw his reflection in her. Her movement changed his attraction to fear.

> I guess it was with a guy that had a habit of looking into every mirror that we passed. I mean, Hello! He was worse then some girls I know!

Narcissists think they're smart and attractive. They can be charming in short-term relationships. Their need for attention can pull a partner along into the limelight. But their need to dominate leads to "game-playing, such as keeping partners uncertain about their commitment, being unfaithful and keeping secrets."[293]

Another narcissist game is thinking your time is more important than your date's. Don't squeeze your date into your busy schedule. You won't impress her. She should think that meeting her is the most important event of your day.

Showing off money is a form of narcissism, or, in this case, showing off expensive wines:

> A bad date is anybody who arrives stoned or drunk or anyone who gets stoned or drunk while on the date. And another bad date is anyone who insists that I go dutch or pay. And another bad date is anybody who tries to kiss me, oh, before dinner. And another bad date is anybody who tries to impress me with what he knows about wines; I think that's really disgusting. And another bad date is anybody who takes you to one of those torturous, four-star restaurants where there're seventeen courses and insist

you try everything. I mean that's hell.[294]

— Rae Dawn Chong, actress

Women prefer men with lots of money, who don't make a big deal about it.

Here's a man who wasn't narcissistic:

> Bart showed up in a clunker car, which was quite a change from my previous boyfriend. My ex- was really into his car. He had a brand-new sports car, and at times I thought he loved his car more than me.
>
> So here's this new guy, Bart, in a really horrid car. He parked on campus, and we were walking toward the theater, when someone yelled, "Hey! Isn't that your car?"
>
> We looked back to see smoke billowing out of the hood. Bart just smiled and said, "I'll deal with it tomorrow," and he kept walking with me. I was blown away! I thought, "He's not overly concerned with his car! He'd rather be with me!"[295]

The couple married. They've been together 13 years.

Inappropriate Touch

For some individuals, touch is enjoyable but "no big deal." These individuals like touching and being touched. They easily learn physical skills, e.g., skiing. Touch and physical movement makes them awake and "in the moment." In contrast, sitting in a lecture sends their minds off to dreamland. On a date, such an individual may happily respond to your touch, but don't assume that he or she wants to have sex.

To other individuals, all touch is intimate. These individuals can't stand being touched by strangers. They have difficulty learning physical skills. Auditory stimulation, e.g., a lecture or concert, makes them awake and attentive. A massage sends them off to dreamland. Movement therapy (e.g., yoga or Feldenkrais) is difficult for them, but produces deep, life-changing feelings.

When dating such an individual, keep your hands to yourself until your date trusts you. When the person is ready, your touch will make him or her feel intensely connected.

If you and your date have conflicting touch styles, discuss each other's needs. It's rude and unpleasant for a casual toucher to be "all over" a person who's sensitive to being touched. But it's equally rude for a touch-sensitive person to make his or her date sit motionless through a two-hour concert, when the date needs to dance or be touched.

To learn more about this, read *The Open Mind,* by Dawna Markova (1991).

Too Focused on Sex

> The worst date I've had I would have to say was with this guy that did not understand the meaning of no. He was trying to get me to bed from the minute we met and did not let up until I pushed him out the door and locked it! Was not a pleasant experience, actually scared me, and I have found I am much more safety conscious now.

> The guy assumed we were going to have sex just because we had discussed sex briefly on the phone. It was our first date! Our first meeting. I kept asking him to stop & slow down. Finally he got the point & left. Needless to say I was glad!!!

If dating were a car, the man has his hands on the steering wheel. The woman has her feet on the accelerator and brake pedals. He decides where they are going. She decides how fast.

Poor Manners

> The first really big thing you learn about the guy you're dating is how he treats waiters and waitresses at a restaurant, and what a huge effect that will have on the rest of the relationship.[296]
> — Edie Falco, who was a waitress for twenty years, and now plays Carmela Soprano on *The Sopranos*

Personal Hygiene

> An unbearable date is one with a man who has body odor, who hasn't brushed his teeth for months, who talks

about his work the whole time, or worse his mother's cooking.

When I'm flatulent at a party, I find the worst-dressed guy and stand next to him.

"Dutch Treat"

A blind date...was highly respectable and highly thought of by my friend. He was (I guess still is) a therapist. He called and we discussed meeting for coffee at a neutral place in the daytime. He was insistent on going out to dinner, that our first date should be a dinner date. He asked me to dinner and he insisted on picking me up at my home. Against my better judgment I consented even though my co-worker assured me he was a "stand up guy" and "okay." We go to dinner and at the end of the meal when the check comes he tallies up what "I owe" and hands me the bill and asked for the money. He told me that every woman he dates pays her own way.

The guy was late picking me up. When he showed up, he looked like he had slept in his clothes. He informed me that we had to take my car because his was in the shop. After dinner, he couldn't pay the bill, and asked if he could borrow the money to pay it. I took him to his place and he tried to get me to stay the night with him. I finally told him where to go, in a polite way.

Any first date that involved coupons.

Too Disorganized

Showing up late, not having dinner reservations or theater tickets, having car trouble—not being in control of your basic life stuff won't get you points.

Too Organized

But being too organized can be as bad:

He had everything planned and rehearsed and nothing

goes right...ugh!

When we were late for any planned event that day, she lost it.

Plan the date, but plan options for your date to choose. Suggest two restaurants, or two movies you'd like to see. Let her choose. If the weather is bad on your hiking trip, have a museum to visit. Spontaneity is romantic.

Violence and Physical Abuse

I had a man that hit me on our first date and that didn't fly at all with me. Let's just say I dropped him off 30 min from his house out in the middle of nowhere. I felt kinda bad, but he hit me so I felt kinda justified.

Out to dinner, date gets drunk, starts fight with stranger, got shot at, and windows busted out of car with bumper jack.

5 Dating Mistakes Women Make

Lying About Boyfriends, Jealous Ex's

The worst date must have been the time her boyfriend showed up at the dinner table. Honestly, I didn't know he existed before the date. Machismo is really funny sometimes. Fortunately, I can laugh about it now. It was probably the closest I've ever come to having someone really kick my butt.

Went out to eat, saw a movie. Then dropped her off, she was tired....As I left her ex-boyfriend pulled up and went inside. The next day I walked by (she was my neighbor) and he was still there. Did not make me feel so good about the date when I saw her that afternoon and she had several fresh hickies on her neck.

I had a date set for a week. We went out. It felt really weird during the date. Afterwards, she told me that she got back with her ex the day before. She still went out with me because she didn't want to break my heart. (Go figure.)

Her "old boy friend" smashed a wooden chair on my back during dinner. But that's not what made it so crappy. She went home with the guy cause I wouldn't "fight" for her.

Women lie about boyfriends. Men lie about wives.

Standing Up Dates

Stood up at the last minute to a Rolling Stones concert.

Getting stood up trying one of those dating services.

I showed up at her door as she was going out with friends. She had forgot all about our date.

Getting stood up is one of the most common complaints from men about women. I've heard no complaints from women about getting stood up by men.

Tell dates to meet you at your office or home. Your date can be late—or not show up at all—and you haven't been inconvenienced.

Negative Attitude

I went out with a woman who was so negative that it ruined my night.

A woman who is not an upbeat person.

Feminine individuals (including feminine men) do picky complaining. Masculine individuals (including masculine women) look for something positive to say about suboptimal situations.

Demanding and Critical

It was a night of hell while I went from bar to bar spending my money on a person I did not want to be with. Most demanding person I have ever met too, demanded drinks, demanded food, demanded everything.

Or she's bored and demands that you take her to more entertaining places. Translation: you're boring.

Going to a hockey game and wanting to leave early when the game is tied or close. I'll give you your bus fare!

Theft
She stole my wallet, clothes, and car.

She stole your clothes? I'd like to hear her side of the story.

SEX

Contraceptives

Many women know little about contraceptives. Of 357 women who sought abortions at the University of Pittsburgh School of Medicine,

- 27% used no contraception at all.
- 31% used birth control incorrectly.
- 21% of women used birth control correctly, "but experienced an event that placed them at risk for pregnancy" (e.g., a condom broke), and then didn't follow up with emergency contraception. "Emergency contraceptives" are hormone pills used within the first 72 hours after sex to prevent pregnancy (brand names include Preven and Plan B). 73% of the women were unaware of emergency contraception.[297]

Everyone—men and women—should have a copy of *Our Bodies, Ourselves*, by the Boston Women's Health Collective (1998). The book includes a 50-page chapter about birth control. If you hesitate to spend $24 on the book, imagine 18 years of child-support payments.

Or find free information about contraceptives on the Johns Hopkins University website, at http://www.reproline.jhu.edu.

Sexually Transmitted Diseases (STDs)

Sexually transmitted diseases (STDs) aren't cured by simply going to a health clinic for a shot. STDs cause health problems long after treatment. E.g., STDs increase risk of prostrate cancer in men.[298] STDs cause infertility and cancer in women. The viral STDs— genital herpes, HPV (causes genital warts and cervical cancer[299]), AIDS—can't be cured.

STDs are equally common across educational, income, age, and racial groups.[300]

STDs aren't limited to young people. Single women over forty are more promiscuous than single young women.[301] Women who divorce after twenty years of marriage can be clueless about condoms.

First Rule: Have Few Sexual Partners

The most effective way to avoid STDs is to have a long-term, monogamous relationship. You'll enjoy the best sex and have the most relationship satisfaction (see "Sexual Satisfaction in Monogamous Relationships," page 48).

Individuals who have had two, three, or four partners have a 3-5% likelihood of contracting a STD. This percentage jumps *ten times* (to 28-35%) for men and women with more than twenty sexual partners.[302]

Each additional partner exposes you to that partner's partners (exposure increases with the square of the number of your partners). E.g., a man who has had sex with two women, each of whom has had sex with two other men, has been exposed to four men. But a man who has had sex with twenty women, each of whom has had sex with twenty men, has been exposed to 400 men.

Promiscuous individuals are more likely to engage in unsafe sex.[303] Only about half use condoms.[304] Promiscuous individuals are more likely to use drugs or alcohol before sex. They're more likely to have sex with prostitutes.[305] They're less likely to seek tests or treatment for STDs.

Second Rule: Avoid Drugs and Drug-Users

Drug use increases risk of STDs in three ways:
- Some drugs suppress the immune system, i.e., cripple your body's natural abilities to fight infections. E.g., cocaine use increases AIDS transmission 200 times.[306] Smoking increases risk of cervical cancer from HPV.[307]
- Individuals who use drugs are more likely to engage in unsafe sex (see "Stress and Promiscuity," page 47). These individuals may trade sex for drugs, or support an addiction via prostitution.

• Intravenous drug users (e.g., heroin addicts) who share needles also share diseases, including hepatitis and AIDS.

Third Rule: Don't Share Bodily Fluids

Nevada's legal brothels have the following three rules:[308]
• No kissing on the mouth.
• No fingers, tongues, etc. in vaginas or other orifices.
• Use condoms, including for oral sex.

But don't assume that a condom alone will keep you safe. Condoms help prevent AIDS and gonorrhea. But researchers aren't sure whether condoms stop HPV, chlamydia, syphilis, or herpes.[309]

Fourth Rule: Get Tested Regularly For STDs.

Check-ups catch diseases before symptoms occur, when the diseases are easier to treat. This is especially important for women —when symptoms occur, permanent reproductive damage may have already occurred.

Get tested with each new partner before you have sex. Get tested again six months later (some STDs take months to show up). Expect to spend $400-500 for an STD test. Some low-income clinics and universities give free STD tests. Results come back from the lab in about three weeks.

Fifth Rule: Ask the Right Questions, at the Right Time

Most people with STDs are symptom-free, unaware of their infections, and untreated.[310] 75% of HIV-positive young gay men (including 91% of HIV-positive African-American young gay men) don't know they're infected.[311]

If they know they have an STD, they won't admit this embarrassing fact. 75% of HIV-positive men and women who know they're infected don't inform casual sex partners.[312]

Between not knowing and not saying, more than 90% of STD-infected people will say "no" if you ask "Do you have any sexually transmitted diseases?"

Instead ask five questions:
• "When was your last STD test? What were the results?"

Don't be embarrassed to ask to see the lab report.
- "How many sexual partners have you had since then?"
- "Did you have sex without a condom with any of these partners?"
- "Do you use intravenous drugs?" Look for needle marks.
- "Were any of your partners gay or bisexual men, or intravenous drug users, in cities with high incidence of AIDS?"

Don't trust a new partner. *Always* use a condom with a new partner.

Don't wait until you're in bed to ask these questions. A lover "ready to go" will impair your judgment. You may also have been drinking. Ask when you have your partner's shirt off, but before your have his or her pants off. If your partner is at risk, say that you'll wait until he or she is tested.

Sixth Rule: Sex Toys

While you wait for your partner's test results, discover the amazing things the two of you can do with sex toys. Read *Good Vibrations: The New Complete Guide to Vibrators*, by Joani Blank (2000).

> There are a number of mechanical devices which increase sexual arousal in women. Among these is the Mercedes-Benz 500SL.
> — Lynn Lavner

AIDS Isn't "Everybody's Disease"

> Many geographic areas and strata of the population are virtually untouched by the [AIDS] epidemic and probably never will be; certain confined areas and populations have been devastated and are likely to continue to be.[313]
> — Albert Jonsen and Jeff Stryker, *The Social Impact of AIDS in the United States* (1993)

AIDS is difficult to transmit. If you have unprotected sex once with an HIV+ partner, you have about a one in 500 chance of infection. The likelihood is more for women and for anal intercourse; less for men (especially circumcised men[314]) or for vaginal intercourse; and much lower when a condom is used. In contrast, the likelihood of getting gonorrhea from an infected partner is about one in two.[315]

AIDS is associated with gay men because some gay men have large numbers of sexual partners. In the early 1980s, gay men with AIDS averaged 1,100 partners.[316] AIDS is geographically concentrated (e.g., in New York and San Francisco) because gay men can find that many partners in only a few cities.

Nevada's legal brothels—where a prostitute may have sex with 1,000 men each year—demonstrate the effectiveness of "safe sex" precautions. In addition to the three rules (listed above) to prevent sharing bodily fluids, Nevada's legal prostitutes are tested monthly for STDs. Brothels also police their prostitutes for intravenous drug addictions. A study of 535 prostitutes in Nevada's legal brothels found that none were HIV-positive. In contrast, studies of Nevada illegal prostitutes ("streetwalkers") found that 6-10% were HIV-positive. The researchers attributed this to intravenous drug addictions.[317]

For more STD information, see:
- The National Institutes of Health fact sheet, at
    http://www.niaid.nih.gov/factsheets/stdinfo.htm
- The Centers for Disease Control STD info, at
    http://www.cdc.gov/nchstp/dstd/dstdp.html

Consent

Age Precludes Consent
In many states, an adult having sex with a 17-year-old is statutory rape or even child molestation. A judge could convict the adult as a sex offender. For the rest of her life she'll have to register with the police. This includes teenage couples a few months apart in age, when the older teenager (either the boy or the girl) turns 18.

Check your state's laws at http://www.ageofconsent.com. The website also lists foreign countries.

Alcohol Precludes Consent

Some universities have policies that students "under the influence of alcohol or drugs are absolutely incapable of giving sexual consent."[318] I.e., if a drunken student has sex and later accuses her partner of unwanted sex, the partner is automatically guilty.

At one university, a drunken female student repeatedly called a sober male student explicitly asking him to come to her room for sex. She later accused the male student of forcing her to have sex. The male student was suspended, then put on probation and required to go to counseling for a year. Other students put signs outside his dorm room saying that he was a rapist.[319]

At another university, two students drank and downloaded pornography from the Internet. The female student then undressed and got into the male student's bed. The next day she told university administrators that the male student had forced her to have sex. The male student was immediately expelled from the university and evicted from his dorm room, without a trial.[320]

In both cases the female accusers—both under 21—weren't punished for violating university alcohol policies. The university administrators implied that drunken female students aren't responsible for their actions, but male students—sober in the first case, drunken in the second case—are responsible for their actions. Such policies are sexist. The policies are analogous to a university allowing drunken female students to vandalize school property, while punishing drunken male vandals.

Such university policies are also misguided in their "zero tolerance" of alcohol. E.g., a student who consumes ten drinks and then collapses in another student's bed is incapable of sexual consent, but a student who consumes one drink and then three hours later wants sex isn't a helpless victim.

A better policy would encourage students to "know their limits" and drink only moderately. Universities could inform students of the direct correlation between number of drinks consumed and level of sexual intimacy on dates (see "Alcohol," page 118) and suggest that students limit their drinking to their desired level of sexual intimacy.

Sexual Harassment

Sexual harassment occurs when an individual with power offers to make a favorable decision in return for sexual activity with the affected individual.[321]

In recent years, courts and employers increased the "gray areas" of sexual harassment. Now, "sexual activity" may include inappropriate touch, talking about sex, displaying sexually suggestive photos, etc. "Favorable decisions" may include non-specific future decisions—i.e., everything a supervisor does. The "individual with power" may include employees of equal or lower rank, or even customers, if supervisors are aware of and allow the sexual activity.

Women on Top

Begin sex with the woman putting the condom on the man, and the woman on top. This should prevent most accusations of rape.

How Parents Should Guide Their Teenagers

When I was in eighth grade, our teacher told us about tigers and sheep. Tigers think for themselves and act independently. Sheep go along with what everyone else is doing. Our teacher asked us to decide whether we would choose to live as a tiger for six months (and then die), or live as a sheep for 99 years. He told the tigers to go to front of the room, and sheep to go to back of the room.

We all got up, moved around, and sat down. I was the only student sitting in the back of the room.

This appears to be a paradox—the tigers followed each other in a herd, and the lone sheep (me) thought and acted independently. It actually shows a mischaracterization the teacher made. The students divided themselves into three groups, not two: leader sheep, follower sheep, and a lone independent tiger.

I remember how I made my decision. I envisioned toughing out six months of ridicule—i.e., not caring what other people thought of me—and then enjoying 98.5 years laughing at the dead tigers. Choosing to be a sheep made me the only tiger. Conversely, choosing to be tigers made everyone else sheep.

Tiger and Sheep Sex

Popular teenage boys want to have sex to prove that they're "alpha" males. Teenage girls want relationships with the most popular boys, so agree to have sex. Then followers emulate these leaders. All these teenagers—the leaders and the followers—are sheep.

A teenage tiger, in contrast, doesn't care whether he or she is popular (a tiger that wanted sheep to like him or her would starve). A teenage tiger decides for him- or herself what's right and what's wrong.

Tiger parents give their teenagers information to make decisions (rather than telling their teenagers how to behave). E.g., a teenage girl reading *Sex in America: A Definitive Survey* (1994) finds that the primary reason girls first have sex is affection for their partners (48%)—but only half of their partners (25%) feel the same affection (boys are more likely to want sex out of curiosity). A teenage tigress will question the motives of a boy who wants to have sex with her.[322]

A teenage boy reading *Sex in America* will learn that sexual activity varies widely between groups of teenagers. Some teenagers have sex early. This is reflected in the average age of first sex for boys dropping from 18.5 in the 1950s to 17.5 in 1994.[323] Yet other groups of teenagers abstain. The percentage of men who were virgins at 20 increased from 1% to over 8% (the percentage of women who were virgins at 20 remained more-or-less constant at 5%).[324] These facts prepare a teenage tiger boy to hear different messages from different groups. He'll be better able to select the group he wants to belong to.

Pre-Teen Friendships, Early Teenage Dating, and Teenage Sex

Boys with mostly female friends are 40% more likely to have sex before 17, compared to boys with mostly male friends. But girls with mostly male friends (e.g., tomboys) are 50% *less* likely to have sex before 17.

Adolescents with older friends are 50% more likely to have sex.

Boys and girls who "go steady" and date at least weekly are most likely (67% likelihood) to have sex before 17. Boys and girls who never date are least likely (26% likelihood) to have sex before 17.

The surprise is among boys and girls who date more than one person. Boys who date more often (at least once per week) are more likely to have sex before 17, compared to boys who date less than once per week (60% vs. 50% likelihood). But girls who date more often are *less* likely to have sex before 17, compared to girls who date less often (47% vs. 54% likelihood).

Also surprising is that a large minority of teenagers—16% of girls and 8% of boys—have sex before 17 without ever dating. Parents who don't allow a teenager to date might stop the teenager from having sex, but the teenager might have sex without a relationship, which may be an emotionally damaging experience.[324]

Parents who want their teenagers—boys or girls—to delay having sex should encourage their children to have male friends (e.g., to play sports or join a science club), to have friends their own age, and to date more than one person (i.e., not "go steady"). These parents should encourage their daughters to date many boys, but discourage their sons from dating many girls. And, more important than any other factor, these parents should discourage alcohol consumption on dates.

Talk to Your Teenagers About Sex

In surveys, parents ranked very low when adolescents were asked, "From whom do you get most of your information about sex?" When asked from whom they would prefer to get information, parents were at the top.
— John Jemmott, University of Pennsylvania

The primary reason parents don't talk to their teenagers about sex is that they don't know much about the subject. Parents know about adult sex, but teenage sex is different—e.g., can you discuss levels of physical intimacy on dates?

When parents take sex education classes, their children have less sexual activity. The parents and children report increased communication about sexual behavior.[325]

The abstinence vs. condoms debate is misguided. Promoting abstinence promotes early marriage, which increases likelihood of divorce. Condoms are associated with promiscuous sex, which no parent or school supports.

Instead, discuss with your teenagers why you favor monogamy and oppose promiscuity. Discuss the stages of monogamy: "going steady," co-habitating (living together), engagement, and marriage. Discuss the ideal age for each. Discuss whether sex is acceptable in each type of monogamous relationship.

Get to Know the Parents in Your Village

Parents should avoid the double-standard of pressuring daughters to avoid sex, and then letting sons do what they want. Pressuring a daughter to delay sex can be ineffective if she's getting pressure from a boy to have sex. Pressuring a son to delay sex is more effective, because few girls pressure boys for sex.

Meet the parents of the children your children date. Ask what messages they've given their children about sex. In ancestral hunter-gatherer clans and agricultural villages, everyone knew everyone else. If a young man and a young woman were interested in each other, the families knew each other and encouraged or discouraged the relationship.

Five Tips for Better Kissing

1) Keep your mouth closed until she kisses you with her mouth open. Don't use your tongue until she puts her tongue in your mouth.

2) Be creative where you kiss. Kiss her cheek, ears, and forehead, not just her mouth. Watch the final scene in the French romantic comedy *Amélie*.

3) The sebaceous glands in the mouth and lips release sexually pleasurable chemicals. Smoking, alcohol (especially beer), breath fresheners, and garlic mask these chemicals, making

you less enjoyable to kiss.[326]

4) The sternocleidomastoid (SCM) muscles run from the bottom of each ear down to the collarbone. Kissing, sucking, or biting the SCM is overwhelmingly pleasurable to most people. Make a joke about your Transylvanian ancestry.

5) Steal the bases slowly, one at a time. Women love foreplay.

> Before you make him the happiest man in the universe…he must spend at least four hours [making] compliments about everything from your eyes/face/hair/outfit and legs to the unbearable sweetness of your disposition. There should also be gifts and refreshments.[327]
>
> — Jill Conner Browne, *The Sweet Potato Queens' Book of Love* (1999)

What Women Want in Bed

Sex makes men feel emotionally intimate. Emotional intimacy makes women feel sexual (see "Emotional Connection," page 27).

Orgasms are less important to women than emotional intimacy. Only 29% of women always have orgasms, yet 72% of women are "very" or "extremely" satisfied with their sex lives.[328]

To sexually satisfy a woman, give her kissing and foreplay. Give her "aural sex," i.e., romantic poetry. She wants to hear you say everything you're feeling, or at least the parts having to do with adoring her.

Focusing on a woman's orgasm can make her *less* satisfied:

> I go over the multiplication tables in my head to help myself come later. I will do anything to be able to have an orgasm at the same time as my girlfriend. How can people say that men are selfish in bed?[329]
>
> — anonymous visitor to ConfideInMe.com

At the moment when she most needs to emotionally connect with him, he's multiplying 11 by 13. His emotional disconnection makes her emotionally disconnect. She doesn't orgasm and doesn't enjoy sex with him.[330]

> Women are emotional creatures, so we're hardwired to want more romantic sex—the kind where you connect on a physical and emotional level.[331]
> — Daylle Deanna Schwartz, *How To Please a Woman In and Out of Bed* (2001)

Twenty thousand women wrote to Ann Landers saying they'd give up intercourse if they could have more hugs and cuddling. If you can figure out what to do with her clitoris, great. If not, give her romance.

The Twenty-Four-Hour Rule

> ...within the first twenty-four hours following [an] act of sex, he must telephone to repeat all the pre-sex compliments that he paid you regarding your eyes/face/hair/outfit and legs, and the unbearable sweetness of your disposition, plus, he should have thought up at least fifteen minutes' worth of new and additional compliments about the act itself.[332]
> — Jill Conner Browne, *The Sweet Potato Queens' Book of Love* (1999)

At least e-mail her a love poem. It's OK to copy one of Shakespeare's sonnets or Rumi's romantic poems.

Men's Talk and Women's Reputations

Men talk about the women they've had sex with. Some men brag. Other men—the Sensitive New Age Guys—find relationships to be emotionally difficult and need to talk about their feelings.

Women want good reputations, i.e., that they don't sleep around. Individual women may or may not prefer the "strong, silent type" of man, but they all want men to be strong and silent after having sex.

❤

BECOMING A COUPLE

Males court. Females choose. This works for most of the animal world, in which fathers have little or no involvement in their offspring.

But women need long-term relationships. Switching from dating to a committed relationship requires switching gender roles. Men must choose whether to stay in a relationship. Women must court their mates to stay committed.

Permanently Passive Women

Women stuck in the passive, *choosing* gender role don't move from dating into a relationship.

E.g., a woman works hard on her clothes and make-up, to attract men. She read *The Rules*, so plays "hard to get." She expects a man to work hard to please her, e.g., give her flowers and gifts and attention. After sex, she wants to be rewarded with more flowers and gifts and attention.

After sex, the man hopes that the relationship will become easier, not harder. He wants her to call and ask him out. He sees other women calling their boyfriends. He thinks that's the way relationships should be.

He's unsure whether she likes him. On the one hand, she has sex with him. On the other hand, she never calls.

He slacks off, waiting for her to call. She thinks he's a cad. He thinks she's lazy and self-centered. The relationship goes into a downward spiral.

Men reject (or cheat on) permanently passive women, no matter how beautiful such a woman is.

Permanent Pursuers

Men stuck in the active, *courting* gender role don't move from dating into a relationship.

A man may enjoy the chase—and then get bored when he catches the object of his desire, and move on. Or he tries to impress women with his sports car and dining at expensive restaurants, but bores them by talking about his car and his career, and the women break off the relationships.

Switch Genders Roles for Commitment

Instead, picture a couple reversing gender roles. She actively guides the direction of the relationship (traditionally into commitment and marriage). He intelligently makes good choices.

E.g., she calls and asks him out. She risks hurt feelings if he says no. If he says "yes," she shows up at his apartment and brings him flowers. She drives him to his softball game. She cheers whenever he hits the ball. Then they go out with his team to a steakhouse. He can drink all the beer he wants, because she's driving. She laughs at his jokes. Then they go back to her apartment, where she makes his favorite dessert. What she's doing is how men normally date women. It's not normal behavior for a woman.

Imagine that the man acts likes a woman. All he has to do is make intelligent choices. He's thinking that the cute young waitress at the steakhouse smiled when he left a big tip. He has to decide whether to commit to a relationship with the woman he's dating, or to break it off and chase other women.

If he thinks like a man, he'll chase the pretty young woman. If he gets her to come home with him, she'll smoke like a chimney, drop corn chips on his carpet, and want to use his computer to read her e-mail while he's trying to seduce her.

If he thinks like a woman, he'll focus on his partner's good qualities. He'll recognize that she makes him happy. He'll realize that her shortcomings are unimportant. This is how women normally look at men. It's not how men normally look at women.

Switching Gender Roles Is Difficult

When dating with stereotypical gender roles, men ask women out. Men risk rejection and embarrassment. Each rejection is an emotional "direct hit." Asking women out takes courage. Courage

—and controlling our emotions—is something men are good at. We can handle rejection and can figure out—most of the time—whether a woman's "no" means "not this weekend, but ask me again next weekend," or means "never in a million years."

When a woman switches gender roles and asks a man out, she's devastated if he says no. When women switch gender roles they're on unfamiliar ground and easily become lost.

Similarly, men who switch gender roles are on unfamiliar ground. Men can easily slip back into stereotyped gender roles—e.g., when seeing a pretty young woman.

When you switch gender roles, tell your partner. E.g., if a woman switches to using masculine behavior, and her man stays with masculine behavior, they'll compete and the relationship will crash. If he switches to feminine behavior, sliding over to the passenger seat, but she doesn't get into the driver's seat, the relationship won't go anywhere.

"Our Relationship" Talks

Have an "our relationship" conversation to make "the switch" from dating to a relationship. Agree on a time and place for the conversation. Don't surprise your partner. Don't work it in while the two of you are doing something else.

Stay in contrasexual gender roles. If you're a woman, talk about where you want to take him. Say this both literally—e.g., "I'd like to take you for a weekend at the beach"—and where you want to take the relationship—e.g., whether you want marriage.

If your man rejects your requests, handle his rejections in the masculine style by asking whether he means "not now, but maybe later" or "never in a million years." E.g., you may learn that he doesn't want marriage now, but he's open to the idea a few years in the future.

If you're a man, tell your woman how much you appreciate her good qualities. Discuss her faults but stay in the feminine style of saying that you can live with her faults.

If she did something that's intolerable to you, don't angrily end the relationship without telling her what she did to anger you. She won't figure out that she did something wrong. You'll be so mad that you'll do something to anger her. Then she'll angrily end the relationship.

The conclusion of an "our relationship" talk should be ways that each partner can be an individual, yet the two of you are a couple. E.g., if your sport is running, go to track workouts together. He runs with the men. She runs with the women. They're always in sight of each other, but each does his or her own workout. For more about *self-differentiation*, see *Passionate Marriage*, by David Schnarch (1997).[333]

Resistance to Commitment

Poor relationship skills are a vicious circle. Poor dating skills make finding a partner difficult. When you find a partner, you're afraid of losing the person. You want a commitment. But your poor relationship skills make your partner unhappy, and unwilling to make a commitment. Your commitment is an empty promise, because no one else wants you.

If you don't have a choice of partners, don't ask for a commitment. Instead, improve your attractiveness. You might attract someone else's attention. Then you can ask your partner for a commitment. Or your partner may find you to be more attractive.

Life Stages Conflict
Young men see life as four stages:
1. Parents and school—no freedom—for 22 years.
2. Freedom. Maybe he'll travel around the world, working odd jobs in exotic locations. Maybe he'll start his own company, taking financial risk. Maybe he'll go to Hollywood, work as a waiter, and break into acting.
3. Marriage and children—again, no freedom for 25 years. He'll have to work long hours in a dull, safe career, to pay for a wife, mortgage, and mini-van.
4. Retirement. Young men don't think that old guys climb mountains, travel around the world, or break into acting.

To men, the adolescent life stage—questing for treasure and a princess—is the most important. This is Life with a capital L. How much a man accomplishes in this act sets the stage for the rest of his life.

Women see the adult life stage—family and community—as what life is all about. A generation ago, young women skipped the adolescent life stage. They went straight from their father's house into marriage. They never received approval for individual accomplishment. This led to anger, repression, or depression.

Young women today want to have an adolescent life stage, but on a smaller scale than men. E.g., a young woman may want to work at a dot-com, when a young man wants to start the company. Young women want to graduate from college, have two or three years of fun with their boyfriends, marry by 25, have a few more years of fun, and become pregnant by 28.

Women want their adolescent life stage to last five years. Men need the adolescent life stage to last as long as it takes to accomplish everything. A man with big dreams—or a man who fails repeatedly—can spend decades in his adolescent life stage. Psychologists call such a man a *puer*, or flying boy (see "Hermes," page 176).

Men don't settle down until they've completed their adolescent life stage. A man needs to page through *Outside* magazine and say, "Been there, done that." Then he needs to page through *Inc.*, *Car & Driver*, and *Playboy* and say the same thing.

A woman who wants commitment should date older men, who've achieved their goals. Or look for a man with small dreams. Or make her man feel that he's accomplished everything he needs to. Or promise him that marriage won't restrict his freedom.

Deciding Whom to Marry vs. Deciding When to Marry

Men, in general, decide when to marry. E.g., a man expects to marry when he's established in his career and owns a home. Whom he marries is a decision requiring less consideration—he proposes to the woman he's going out with when he's ready to marry.

Women, in general, decide whom to marry. Women expect to meet Prince Charming, fall in love, and live happily ever after.

When men choose whom to marry, they often handle the decision badly. E.g., a man who attracts many women prefers to have several casual relationships instead of switching to feminine sexuality and one monogamous relationship. Or a man who rarely attracts women is unable to tell the rare woman who wants him how much he needs her.

Conversely, men have difficulty deciding not to get involved with women that they're not seriously interested in, if the women want them.

Women have difficulty choosing when to marry. E.g., a woman who wants a family feels increasing anxiety as she approaches 30 without having met Prince Charming. Unlike a man, she doesn't automatically marry whomever she's going out with when she's ready to marry.

Conversely, women have difficulty choosing when to break off a relationship. E.g., a woman moves in with the first man she sort of likes, and hopes that over time he'll improve (see "Boyfriend Lies," page 69). Or she settles for a man whom she really likes, and accepts a suboptimal relationship—e.g., he lives in another city, or is involved with another woman—and hopes that the relationship improves. Ten years later, these women have invested so much time that they don't want to "cut their losses" and break off their relationships.

Women should instead think more about when they want to marry, and less about whom they want to marry. Women have a relatively narrow time window to marry. Marrying before 26 is unwise because most individuals develop stable adult identities only after 26 (see "Developing an Adult Identity," page 78). But women who want families should marry by 30, or risk increasing infertility. Additionally, women become less attractive to men as they age (see "Youth," page 23). Because women prefer to marry older men, fewer unmarried men are available as women age (see "Man Shortage or Woman Shortage?" page 93). 28 to 30 is the ideal age for women to marry, depending on each individual woman's maturity and how many children (if any) she desires.

If you're a woman, estimate how many men you've dated in your lifetime. Set a goal to date this many men from now until the date you propose. I.e., use masculine sexuality, dating many potential partners (this doesn't mean having sex with many partners). Pick the best man and ask him to marry you (that's right—*you* propose). If you're over 25 and set at least two years for this dating period, you're statistically unlikely to meet a better partner after you've married.[334]

Men should decide whom they want to marry. Don't get involved with women whom you don't want to marry. They'll try to stop you from dating other women. Wait until you meet a woman with whom you feel, "I could marry this woman." Then tell her that—even if it's on the first date. Don't try to have casual sex with her or play other games (i.e., you should use feminine sexuality, wanting a monogamous relationship). If she's hesitant, tell her that you'll wait until she's ready—even if you have to wait ten years.

CONFLICT IN RELATIONSHIPS

Unresolved conflict wastes our time and energy, but resolving conflict makes us better off than we were before the conflict. If we never conflicted, we'd never change, achieve, create, or grow.

Conjunct Relationships

Partners who agree about everything can make each other miserable. E.g., you're fired from your job. You tell your partner that you'll never amount to anything. Your partner agrees. That isn't what you need to hear!

The myth: All relationship problems stem from conflict.

Reality: If both partners are miserable, they're not in conflict. The partners should work on disagreeing. Conflict will help them grow to a new life stage, in which they're no longer miserable.

Opposite Relationships

In an *opposite* relationship, if you come home in an extreme emotion, e.g., despair, your partner responds with the opposite emotion, e.g., hope. If you lost your job, your partner says that you'll get a better job.

Or you win big in Las Vegas. You feel happy. Without a partner, or with a conjunct partner, you'll place another bet. You don't need a Ph.D. in statistics to know that if you continue to bet, sooner or later you'll lose. But your opposite partner recognizes your overconfidence, and suggests that you quit while you're ahead. You agree, and take your partner out to a romantic restaurant.

Handled well, opposite partners pull each other from emotional extremes to the emotionally neutral center. There each can shift to another emotion. If an opposite relationship is unhappy, try to compromise.

Romantic movies begin with opposite individuals. She's Donald

Trump's personal assistant. He's a foot-long hot dog vendor. Over time they grow to appreciate and love each other. We enjoy romantic movies because we recognize that opposite relationships are ideal for two individuals.

The myth: Agreement is the basis of happy relationships.

Reality: Opposites attract—and create balanced, emotionally healthy relationships.

Triangular Relationships

Think of a three-person relationship you've been in. You had adventures together, bouncing ideas off each other that no one individual would have thought of. Together you felt balanced.

Now recall how you felt with one of these partners, when the third partner was missing. You felt connected to your partner, but in an oblique way. You didn't agree, yet you didn't openly conflict. While such a relationship looks peaceful on the outside, it's confusing for the partners. Attempts to bring the relationship closer misfire, as if each partner can't see exactly where the other is. They can't pull each other to the emotionally neutral center.

E.g., Joe loses his job and comes home feeling down. Mary is watching her favorite television show. Joe sits down with her, but can't get his mind off his troubles. He doesn't want to disturb her so doesn't say anything. Mary notices that Joe is fidgety, but figures that if something is bothering him he'll say something. She continues to enjoy her television show. No conflict occurs, but neither partner's emotions change.

Their third roommate, Chris, comes home. Chris isn't interested in Mary's television show, and notices that Joe seems down. Chris mentions this to Mary. Mary switches off the television, and all three sit down to talk. Together they balance and reach the neutral center. If two individuals are in an unhappy triangular relationship, find the missing third partner.

The myth: The only "real" relationships have two partners.

Reality: A three-person relationship can be as happy and effective as a two-person relationship.

Square Relationships

When two individuals' personalities relate *squarely*, the partners are at cross-purposes. The partners expend energy fighting each other. The relationship goes nowhere and produces nothing.

Including a third side of the square changes the heat into light. The energy of the two fighting partners produces creative, innovative achievement for the third partner.

Including the fourth side of the square stops the fighting. The partners' energy now goes entirely to creativity and achievement.

E.g., when I was in graduate school, four classmates and I did a six-month consulting project with a manufacturing company. My classmates agreed about everything. I didn't. Our clients agreed with me. Our professors agreed with my classmates. The four sides of the square were my classmates, me, the client (300 managers and employees), and the two professors.

When we five students got together, we'd verbally fight for hours, day after day, getting nowhere. My classmates even once threatened to beat me up.

The clients disliked my classmates, and avoided working with them. A client manager once threatened to beat up one of my classmates.

But when my classmates and I worked with our clients, we achieved tremendous results. Near the end of the project, we met with seven other teams of students working with other companies. The other teams (all of which had 12 students) had little or no conflict. They reported minor, superficial results. When we reported what we were doing, jaws dropped across the audience. Afterwards, students enviously asked how the five of us had accomplished so much.

Looking back, I wish we'd involved the professors more. On the few occasions when the professors were with us, we didn't fight.

Symbolically, the vertical axis represents the connection between heaven and earth, i.e., our inner connection to spirit. The horizontal axis represents our connection to other people. A square relationship can connect us to other people while helping us grow.

The myth: Compromise solves all problems.

Reality: Stand your ground, but bring additional partners into the relationship.

More reality: A couple can relate differently in different areas of their lives. E.g., a couple might share a hobby, have opposite careers, live with a third person, and participate in a square community relationship (e.g., a school's parents, teachers, administrators, and students).

Larger Groups

Larger groups also can pull an individual from an emotional extreme to the emotionally neutral center. When relationships push women to emotional extremes, they turn to their friends for support.

Men, in contrast, don't talk to other men about their problems. But this is the value of *men's issues groups.* When men overcome their reluctance and go to a meeting, much comes out. Because of the emotional intensity men experience in these groups, and the resulting personal and spiritual growth, men's groups are often held in churches (e.g., Promise Keepers). Men's groups can also be located through your university or on your newspaper's community events page. (Don't just use an online men's issues group. Talking to each other face-to-face is important—and you might actually like the group hug at the end of the meeting.)

Or start a relationships books reading group at a bookstore café. Ask the bookstore to put your meetings on their calendar of events. Plan a meeting to discuss personal ads, and ask a newspaper's personal ads section to advertise the meeting free. Invite psychologists or your favorite author—me, of course!—as guest speakers. Announce your group on

http://www.FriendshipCenter.com/hearts

Dyad Trouble

A *dyad* is the personality of a couple. When your friends refer to you and your partner as "Betty-and-Bob," as if the two of you were one person, you've become a dyad.

Adolescents don't handle dyads well. A young man who hasn't proven himself in the world—i.e., hasn't developed a strong individual personality—feels threatened by the compromises necessary to form a dyad with his girlfriend.

Young women, in general, are happy to lose themselves in a dyad. But a man can easily manipulate a young woman who lacks a strong individual personality. The young woman may do things against her self-interest, to benefit her partner. She strengthens her dyad personality to make up for her lack of individual personality. If this weakens her individual personality, she goes into a downward spiral. Her growing dyad personality pushes out her individual personality, until she has no individual will.

> A man is more likely to let the relationship suffer to hold on to his sense of self, while a woman is more apt to let her identity suffer to help strengthen it.[335]
> — David Schnarch, *Passionate Marriage* (1997)

Young men do this too. E.g., military units eliminate soldiers' individual personalities, substituting the group personality. Recruits are taught that individually they are nothing, but the group they compose is strong.

These gender roles reverse after 40. Older men enjoy losing their individuality in a dyad. Older women enjoy independence.

Staying in Relationships

Two-thirds of unhappily married couples that stay together report happiness five years later. The unhappier the couple, the more likely they are to be happy five years later, if they stay together.

Unhappily married couples who divorce and unhappily married couples who stay together are, five years later, equally happy.[336]

Sometimes an individual blames his or her spouse for his or her unhappiness, when he or she has a deeper, hidden cause of unhappiness. Divorce doesn't solve these individuals' problems.

Divorce sometimes creates problems. Divorce sets in motion events over which the individuals have little control—reactions of children or relatives, or difficulty finding or maintaining a new relationship.

> "In two years you will be in a similar room, packing in a similar way, walking out on the next guy, and then two years after that on the next one, and one day you'll look back and say, 'What do I have to show for the last ten years?'"
>
> I kept throwing my clothes and [our daughter's clothes] into the suitcase in one big jumble.
>
> "But," Aaron went on, "you could stay and work this out with me, and in ten years you'll look back and you'll say 'I preserved this family,' and that will be the thing you will be most proud of, no matter what else you do with your life."
>
> I stopped, frozen by the clarity of what he had said about me. There aren't many times in your life you hear a truth so piercing. There was no attack, just a simple assessment of my future.
>
> When the cab came, he sent it away. We talked, we cried, and we agreed to try. It's nineteen years later, and it is the thing I am most proud of.[337]
>
> — Lesley Stahl, *Reporting Live* (2000)

As a child, you didn't accept responsibility for your failures. When you act like a child, you blame your partner for your issues. Then you repeat the problem in the next relationship. You blame all men or all women for having the same problem.

In the adolescent life stage, your relationships fail, but you expect points for trying. This is better, but you're not ready for marriage.

In the adult life stage, you accept your partner's faults and value her strengths. You stay together even when a relationship isn't perfect. You may also stay together because your children's happiness is more important than your own happiness.

Couples stuck between the adolescent and adult life stages criticize and nag each other. They're consciously determined to stay together (adult life stage), but express unhappiness in ways that makes the partner aware of his or her failure (adolescent life stage). Or, worse, a spouse uses childhood finality to express unhappiness (e.g., "You never do anything right.").

> Couples who are destined for divorce start out an argument in anger, criticize, show contempt for each other, and act defensively. When one tries to make peace, the other refuses. Quite often one (usually the woman) will [emotionally] overwhelm the other, who withdraws emotionally....Over months and years of arguing like this, couples amass so many bad memories that one or both of them just give up.[338]
> — Norman Rosenthal, *The Emotional Revolution* (2002)

Consumer Reports found that marital counseling received the lowest ratings, compared to patients seeking help for other problems. Only about 35% of couples experience long-term benefit form marital counseling.[339]

In general, marital counseling help couples who are experiencing communication problems. But psychologists are notorious for only working on communication problems, and ignoring other issues.

ARCHETYPES

EMOTIONAL CONTROL SYSTEMS

Reptiles—and unemotional people—always react the same way to events. Mammals, in contrast, select from a variety of reactions. *Emotions* enable flexible responses to environmental stimuli.[340]

Emotional control systems are hardwired into mammalian brains.[341] Neuroscientists have identified ten emotional control systems. These emotions are:

- Seeking and anticipation; energetic, goal-directed searches for food, shelter, mates, etc.
- Homeostasis—balance of oxygen, water, temperature, etc. —and the discomfort of deprivation and pleasure of relief.
- Anger and rage, when another animal takes our resources (food, shelter, mate).
- Fear, and fearful anticipation of the future.
- Separation distress, e.g., when a mother and child lose each other. This is the basis of *anxiety* and *panic*.
- Sexuality and lust.
- Nurturance and maternal behavior.
- Fun, joy, and playing to create social bonds.
- Sorrow, grief, and loneliness.
- The sense of self.

These neural pathways are the basis of personality types. While everyone has all ten emotional control systems, different circuits are stronger or weaker in different individuals. A neural pathway that an individual uses often becomes *myelinated* or stronger.[342] E.g., a mother develops strong maternal instincts.

An individual's personality type is the emotional control

system she uses most often. One of the goals of personal growth is to strengthen underused emotional control systems. An immature individual responds to all events with the same emotion.

Archetypes

Personality types repeat in human experiences generation after generation. These *archetypes* appear in the ancient world as gods and in myths and folktales.[343] Archetypes appear in the modern world as celebrities, movie formulas, and recurring news events.

The above ten emotional control systems, plus several speculative circuits, form the fifteen personality types in the following chapters. The speculative emotional control systems are
- Valuing the past through tradition, ritual, and ceremony (Hera).
- Homemaking (Hestia).
- Skillful use of tools, especially controlling fire (Hephaestus).
- The quest for meaning (Dionysus).

Additionally, Poseidon symbolizes the limbic brain not integrated with the cerebral cortex, and Apollo symbolizes the reverse.

Individuals embody different archetypes at different life stages. E.g., a young woman may embody Aphrodite, the goddess of romantic love and feminine beauty. In her 30s, she becomes Demeter, the mother. Later she embodies Hestia, making a beautiful home. Or she may pursue a career, embodying Athena.

The transition between archetypes can be difficult. E.g., an Artemis woman

> ...in her twenties and thirties may resent her suitors and keep them at a distance or choose only those who would never qualify as lifelong partners. For her, dating partners may be temporary liaisons to share an adventure, men who need a lot of distance, or female lovers. Then, in her forties, she may be shocked to find herself feeling lonely and depressed as Artemis recedes from center stage, her developmental needs may suddenly contradict the ruling archetype, requiring emergence of a new pattern, such as Demeter, the goddess of motherhood. If

her ego remains identified with the old pattern, this transition can be confusing and painful.[344]
— Connie Zweig and Steve Wolf, *Romancing the Shadow*
(1997)

Opposites Attract

Similar personalities cause marital problems. E.g., Artemis and Ares look similar, but competition drives the couple apart. The easy road to divorce is to match your spouse's archetype.

In a successful relationship, a partner responds to his partner by selecting an emotion opposite to her emotional state (see "Opposite Relationships," page 146). But opposite personalities are immediately painful. E.g., your wife embodies Hestia and buys every item in Martha Stewart's catalog. You embody Hermes and suggest taking a vacation—hopping freight trains. You'll argue and disagree. But handled well you'll "get on like a house on fire." In the long term, this will produce a happy marriage—and balanced individuals.

Encourage your spouse to embody your opposite archetype. You embody his opposite. E.g., an Athena woman who married an Apollo man (similar personality types) should develop her Artemis energy (his opposite). He should develop his Poseidon side (her opposite). But don't do this at the same time—Artemis and Poseidon don't match.

Ideally, a couple uses all fifteen archetypes, at different times. But most couples stay with a few main archetypes. You need a village of relationships to use all the archetypal pairs.

ZEUS–HERA

Zeus

"President Bill Clinton plays the saxophone presented to him by Russian President Boris Yeltsin," Novoya Ogarova Dacha, Russia, January 13, 1994. Photo by Bob McNeely.[345]

Celebrities

John F. Kennedy, William Shatner (Captain Kirk on *Star Trek*), Alan Alda, Bill Clinton, Boris Yeltsin, Jesse Jackson, Sean Connery.

Hairstyle

A full head of hair, graying at the temples.

Shoes

$300 polished black Allen-Edmonds.

Favorite Movie

The Godfather, starring Marlon Brando (1972).

Mythology

Hades, Poseidon, and Zeus drew lots for their kingdoms. Zeus got the sky, Poseidon the seas, and Hades the underworld. They agreed to share the earth. Instead, Zeus dominated the earth and the humans who later inhabited it. The Romans knew Zeus as Jupiter.

Emotional Control System

The *sense of self* enables power, freedom, and dominance. Too little Zeus energy causes impotence or passive-aggression.

Life Purpose

Zeus, Poseidon, and Hades were the "alpha" males of the Greek pantheon. Zeus men conform to society's rules. A Zeus man seeks a public identity—usually a career—that matches his inner sense of self-importance.

Shadow

Zeus men are status-seekers. A Zeus man may use deception to create the appearance of success. He may sacrifice his subordinates. He may claim credit for another person's work. He may blame another person for his failures.

As the sky god, Zeus saw in wide overviews. He didn't have his feet on the ground. Zeus men can be ungrounded, out of touch with reality. They believe in positive thinking. They tune out negative facts and feelings. E.g., employees say that a "reality distortion field" surrounds Steve Jobs.

A Zeus man may work for years to achieve success, then find that it's not what he expected. He spends his life climbing a mountain—then realizes that he climbed the wrong mountain.

Other Personality Type Systems

Zeus is represented in astrology by Capricorn (integrity, or matching one's personal nature with one's public identity), the 10th House (of Career), and the planet Jupiter. Zeus is Enneagram personality type #3, the Status-Seeker.

Sex

Zeus had sex with any beautiful woman he fancied—and paid the price with a jealous and vengeful wife. Zeus men keep mistresses. But Zeus men aren't great lovers. Their focus on power stunts their emotional maturity.

Meeting

To meet Zeus men, be young and beautiful and have a rich and powerful father.

Hera

As far as I am concerned, I never really lived until I met Ronnie. Oh, I know that this is not the popular admission these days....But Ronnie is my reason for being happy. Without him, I'd be quite miserable and have no real purpose or direction in life.

— Nancy Reagan

Nancy Reagan[346]

Celebrities

Nancy Reagan, Kathie Lee Gifford.

Hairstyle

Big hair. Sleeps in rollers.

Shoes

Anne Klein slingbacks.

Favorite Movie

The Stepford Wives, starring Katherine Ross (1975).

Mythology

Hera was the wife of Zeus. She jealously and cruelly persecuted Zeus's lovers and their children. The Romans knew Hera as Juno.

Emotional Control System

Hera energy is about tradition, ritual, and ceremony.

Life Purpose

A Hera woman's life purpose is to embody her culture's traditions. She uses awareness of the past to create group cohesion. She makes individuals feel they are part of a group by reminding them what the group did in the past.

Shadow

Women who embody Hera often marry doctors, lawyers, or other successful men. But they don't really love their husbands. They love being a successful wife.

Hera women love children who behave properly. But when their children don't fit their ideals, Hera women disconnect or even abandon their children. E.g., look at Nancy Reagan and her non-relationships with daughter Patti and son Ronnie.

Too much Hera energy makes an individual a caricature of whom she thinks she is. Too little makes an individual not take anything seriously.

Some women today reject Hera. They remember their mothers in the 1950s or 1960s, dependent and self-sacrificing. But pushing Hera into the shadow can cause a woman to feel emptiness, or incompleteness. Such a woman should consciously bring Hera's rituals into her life, in ways that don't betray her ideals.

Other Personality Type Systems

Hera is represented in astrology by Libra (balancing two people or forces) and the 7th House (of Marriage and open enemies). Hera is Enneagram personality type #3, the Status-Seeker.

Sex

To Hera women, sex is part of marriage.

Meeting

To meet Hera women, make lots of money. Then join a country

club, go to art museum benefits, and other society events.

Zeus–Hera Marriage

A Zeus–Hera marriage tempers power with tradition. A couple that successfully uses this energy increases their social status.

Zeus

Zeus men see women as either marriageable—beautiful daughters of wealthy, prominent families—or women for sex. They use marriage in their rise to power, e.g., marrying the boss's daughter. Once in power, they go for the beautiful young nymphs.

Hera

Hera women subscribe to wedding magazines. A Hera woman's wedding is the most important day of her life.

A Hera woman may mistakenly marry an Apollo man. Apollo men aren't leaders. She'll push him into a CEO position in which he'll fail, when he would've been a successful vice-president. She'll ruin his career and then divorce him.

Under Stress

Under stress, Zeus and Hera becomes Dionysus. When "the going gets tough," a Zeus man or Hera woman loses emotional coldness and distance. A wounded, human side comes out. At best, he becomes a hero—and becomes sexy to women. She becomes a "real person"—and sexy to men.

At worst, a Zeus man or a Hera woman becomes hysterical, or turns to another side of Dionysus—alcohol.

When Safe

When safe, Zeus and Hera becomes Poseidon. They continue to be "alpha," but "lets their hair down" and show emotions.

POSEIDON–ATHENA

Poseidon

William Halsey[347]

> Before we're through with 'em, the Japanese language will be spoken only in hell![348]
> — William Halsey, Admiral of the Pacific, December 8, 1941

Celebrities

George S. Patton, Che Guevara, Fidel Castro, Jack Kerouac, Jerry Lee Lewis, Bob Dylan, Bob Marley, Larry Flynt.

Hairstyle

Not recently cut—a roughneck.

Shoes

Cowboy boots.

Favorite Movie

Death Wish, starring Charles Bronson (1974).

Mythology

Poseidon ruled the seas. He was discontent that Zeus controlled the earth. Poseidon repeatedly—and always unsuccessfully—

rebelled against Zeus. The Romans knew Poseidon as Neptune.

Poseidon's sons were monsters—giant Cyclops. But father and sons were loyal to each other. After Odysseus blinded Poseidon's son Polyphemus, Poseidon vindictively pursued Odysseus for 20 years.

Poseidon's animal was the horse. Horses symbolize masculine emotions. The prairies are like oceans. Cowboys are Poseidon men.

Emotional Control System

Poseidon symbolized intense, irrational emotions—limbic emotion unmediated by cerebral cortex cognition.

Life Purpose

A Poseidon man's life purpose is to lead a band of rebels. He needs friends who are loyal to him, but rebellious against society's rules.

Poseidon men experience deeper emotions than other men. Other men express emotions as if they're splashing in the waves at the beach. Poseidon men experience the depths of the soul. Poseidon men can be great artists or poets.

Poseidon energy is the "wild man" of the mythopoetic men's movement. The women's movement is about careers, power, and justice. The men's movement is about feeling and expressing emotions. The wild man is instinctive, untamed, and in touch with nature. Robert Bly, in his book *Iron John*, shows contemporary men how to get in touch with their wild man. Bly shows how to use this strength to become a courageous and loving man.

Shadow

Poseidon men live in two worlds: the ocean depths of emotion, and the dry land of society. A Poseidon man lives in the civilized world by repressing his emotions and presenting a calm, smooth surface. But sooner or later his bottled-up emotions become a furious storm.

> Kurt [Cobain] was a complicated, contradictory misanthrope....He professed in many interviews to detest the exposure he'd gotten on MTV, yet he would call his man-

agers to complain when the network didn't play his videos often enough. He planned every musical or career direction, writing out ideas in his journals years before he was able to execute them. Yet, as soon as he was bestowed the honors he had sought, he acted as if they were a terrible inconvenience. He was a man of imposing will, yet he was equally driven by a powerful self-hatred.[349]

— Charles R. Cross

Poseidon men resent Zeus men. E.g., a Poseidon man may experience disaster when he attempts to run a business. And Poseidon men aren't good losers. Zeus men believe that they play by the rules—with the help of Apollo lawyers—and win fair and square. But a Poseidon man who doesn't understand the rules feels that he was cheated.

Under Stress

Under stress, Poseidon becomes Zeus. When "the going gets tough," Poseidon men seek power and status—and often fail. E.g., on March 30, 1981, a mentally ill gunman shot President Ronald Reagan. Vice-President George H. W. Bush was in an airplane.

There was chaos in the press room....[Secretary of State Alexander] Haig went directly to the rostrum. Until that moment he had been intensely focused on the crisis and had been steady, although testy and combative. Now I could see his knuckles turn white as he grasped the lectern; his arms shook and his knees began to wobble.

PRESS REPRESENTATIVE: Who is making the decisions for the government right now?

HAIG: As of now, I am in control here, in the White House.[350]

The Constitution passes control to the Vice-President, and then to the Congress.[351] Americans ridiculed Haig for his gaffe. He suddenly resigned several months later. (Haig now is "in control" of infomercials in Boca Raton, Florida.)

When Safe
When safe, Poseidon becomes Dionysus. Find Poseidon cowboys down at the honky-tonk, imbibing libations to Dionysus, selecting emotionally wounded country-western songs on the jukebox, and attracting women.

Other Personality Type Systems
Poseidon is represented in astrology by Aquarius (rebellion) and the 11th House (of Friends). Poseidon is Enneagram personality type #6, the Devil's Advocate.

Sex
Poseidon men bring emotional intensity to sex. This can be good, but can also be bad for a woman who doesn't want sex.

Meeting
To meet Poseidon men, take up sailing, get a horse, or go to a blues club.

Athena

Hillary Clinton[352]

Celebrities
Judges, prosecutors, executives, teachers.

Hairstyle
Athena wore a helmet. Athena women wear their hair styled to look like a helmet.

Shoes
Low-heeled pumps.

Favorite Television Series
The X-Files, starring Gillian Anderson.

Mythology

Athena was the goddess of cities, military and political strategy, and crafts (e.g., weaving, pottery, metalsmithing). She protected and advised heroic men, e.g., Perseus, Jason, Odysseus, and Heracles (Hercules). The Romans knew Athena as Minerva. Her animal was the owl.

Emotional Control System

Fearful anticipation of the future. Athena was born wearing armor. Athena energy is worry, fear, vigilance, and defense. Athena is active when you put on a helmet for a bike ride, change the battery in your smoke detector, and lock your door at night. Too little Athena energy is reckless or "happy go lucky."

Life Purpose

An Athena woman's life goal is perfection. She's judgmental, critical, conscientious, clean, thrifty, and efficient. She expresses criticism, but her criticism of others is minor compared to her inner self-criticism.

Things have to be a certain way. "Love" and "perfect" merge. She expects to feel love only in a perfect relationship, in a perfect home.

Shadow

Overactive Athena energy becomes paranoia or phobia.

Ethics problems. Athena women can't stand people who break the rules. This isn't the same as being ethical—ethics require compassion. Athena women will follow (or enforce) the rules even when the result is unethical. E.g., in 1979, Hillary Clinton earned $100,000 profit on a $1,000 investment in cattle futures.[353] She never suspected that her brokers were making fraudulent trades to bribe her husband. She didn't break any rules, but allowed questionable conduct to happen around her.

The Medusa effect. Medusa was a monster with serpents instead of hair. Her gaze turned people into stone. Athena helped Perseus kill Medusa. Then Athena used Medusa's head as one of her symbols. Athena women can intellectually dissect an opponent, making the person feel she is "turning to stone" and unable to think or speak. Athena women can take the life out of a party or conversation. The "Medusa effect" can destroy a relationship.

Gender problems. Athena girls consider other girls to be silly. They prefer to play with boys. Athena killed her childhood friend Pallas (granddaughter of Poseidon and Amphitrite) in a competitive game. Similarly, Athena women's competitiveness can kill their friendships with other women. Athena executives can be unsupportive of other women, especially lower-status women such as secretaries. But, as Athena grieved for Pallas, Athena women later grieve for their lost friendships.

"Ladies Against Women." Athena supported Orestes in his trial for murdering his mother Clytemnestra. This symbolized the new patriarchy succeeding the old matriarchy. Athena women defend men against women's interests. E.g., Phyllis Schlafly led the 1970s fight against the Equal Rights Amendment. Athena women support feminist principles as long as the issue is workplace equality. Don't expect support for other feminist issues.

Lack of nurturing. Athena mothers hire nannies to raise their children. They'd rent surrogate mothers to produce the babies, if they could. They can be good mothers of competitive, extroverted, intellectual children—but not of sensitive, physical, or emotional children.

Under Stress

Under stress, Athena women become Hestia. They become melodramatic. Gardening, nature, children, and pets help them reduce stress. They see in these creatures purity, without rules or judgment.

When Safe

When safe, Athena women become Hermes or Aphrodite. With friends they become charming and happy. They like weekend "New Age" personal growth retreats, if the messages from the gods are upbeat.

Other Personality Type Systems

Athena is represented in astrology by Taurus (security) and the 2nd House (of Money). Athena is Enneagram personality type #1, the Judge.

Sex

Athena was one of the three virgin goddesses.[354] Athena women like men and are happiest in professional relationships with men. But keep your hands to yourself—she doesn't want the emotional entanglements of sex.

Meeting

To meet Athena women, go to professional conferences.

Poseidon–Athena Marriage

A Poseidon–Athena marriage tempers emotions with prudence. A couple that successfully uses this energy express feelings without getting into trouble.

Poseidon

Poseidon wanted to marry the sea nymph Amphitrite. He tried to dominate her. She didn't want to marry him, and fled. She agreed only when Poseidon sent a dolphin to talk to her. Poseidon men should work on their ability to communicate with women—or ask a friend to talk for them.

Athena

Athena women go for heroes—e.g., Perseus, Jason, Odysseus, Heracles. Sensitive, compassionate, romantic men don't attract Athena women. They want powerful "alpha" males, preferably waving swords.

Athena women typically marry Zeus men, e.g., Hillary and Bill Clinton. Statues of Zeus and Athena show her standing guard beside her seated king. But this isn't a good marriage choice. The Athena woman will endlessly defend her husband's mistakes—

including his endless philandering.[355]

Another bad marriage choice is an Apollo man. They'll have lousy sex.

Athena women should marry Poseidon men—but only *heroic* Poseidon men. E.g., a businesswoman should marry a cowboy. One of Athena's gifts to humanity was the bridle, to control horses.[356] He'll keep her emotions active, i.e., stop her from "living in her head." She'll keep him integrated into society, i.e., employed and out of jail. E.g., Athena restrained Achilles from drawing his sword in anger against his leader, Agamemnon. Expect titanic battles, but in the long run they'll balance and mature.

Athena–Poseidon romances are a popular movie and television theme—the cool businesswoman and the troubled-but-passionate man. E.g., on *Cheers*, Sam and Diane's on-again, off-again romance entertained viewers for five years. In *Broadcast News* (1987), Athena news producer Holly Hunter chooses between Apollo reporter Albert Brooks and Poseidon news anchor William Hurt. In *The Abyss* (1989), Ed Harris plays a cowboy-style foreman on a sea floor oil drilling rig. Events bring his ex-wife, an engineering manager played by Mary Elizabeth Mastrantonio, to his undersea palace.

APOLLO–ARTEMIS

Apollo

"General Maxwell Taylor (left) and Secretary of Defense Robert McNamara (center) meet with President John F. Kennedy to give him appraisal of the situation in South Viet Nam. The two returned from a close-up inspection of the guerilla war in Viet Nam," October 2, 1963.[357]

Celebrities

Robert McNamara, Leonard Nimoy (Spock) on *Star Trek*; George H. W. Bush, law professors and legal scholars.

Hairstyle

Short, from a barber named Frank who talks about sports.

Shoes

$150 tasseled loafers.

Favorite Television Series
Masterpiece Theater every Sunday night on PBS.

Mythology
Apollo was the Sun god, the lawgiver, and the god of art, music, and poetry. With the motto "Nothing in excess," this was art of good taste and moderation.

Apollo became god of prophecy after killing the oracular serpent Python. This symbolized an archaic goddess of prophecy superseded by the rule of law. Today we use laws to make prophecies, e.g., "If you park in that handicapped space you'll get a ticket." Or we use Oracle® computer databases to predict everything from elections to economics.

Emotional Control System
The right hemisphere of the cerebral cortex processes new information. It's connected to the limbic brain, and so we incorrectly say that emotions are "right brain." Saying that the right hemisphere is more *holistic* is more accurate.

The left hemisphere, in contrast, analyzes information and creates logic, associations, and abstractions. Language is produced in the left hemisphere. The left hemisphere develops later in utero than the right hemisphere, and is thought to have evolved later.[358]

The left hemisphere is poorly connected to the limbic and reptilian brains. Individuals who embody Apollo live the "life of the mind," unconnected to their emotions or bodies.

New ideas usually arise from a person with all three brain systems integrated. Apollo men dislike new ideas. They prefer the classics, which can be appreciated solely with one's left hemisphere.

Life Purpose
Like the Sun, an Apollo man's life purpose is to illuminate the darkness, via clear thinking following abstract principles. These men shine. They're "bright."

Shadow

Apollo was Zeus's son. Apollo men function best as vice-presidents or the "right hand man" of a powerful leader. These men aren't leaders.

Apollo men observe events without getting emotionally involved. Their lives can become detached or compartmentalized. They dislike spontaneity. They want to see a schedule before committing to attend an event. They like to read a book—or every book on a subject—before beginning a project.

Under Stress

Under stress, Apollo becomes Demeter. When the going gets tough, an Apollo second-in-command takes care of the subordinates that the Zeus leader forgets about.

When Safe

When safe, Apollo men become Artemis/Ares/Hephaestus. Their hobbies are goal-directed, e.g., collecting stamps. Apollo men are sports fans. They can work hard when they feel safe.

Other Personality Type Systems

Apollo isn't represented in astrology. Apollo is Enneagram personality type #5, the Observer.

Sex

Schedule it into his Daytimer or it won't happen.

Meeting

Go to business school. You'll meet many bright, capable Apollo men—but you might not be able to tell one from another.

Artemis

Amelia Earhart[359]

Celebrities
"Jo" in *Little Women*, Amelia Earhart, Gloria Steinem, Aretha Franklin, Jane Fonda, *Princess Mononoke*, Nike ads for women.

Hairstyle
Short, windblown.

Shoes
Athletic shoes, hiking boots.

Favorite Movie
Alien, starring Sigourney Weaver (1979).

Mythology
Artemis roamed the wilderness with her band of nymphs and her pack of dogs. As a hunter and an archer, her arrows always hit her target. Women who embody Artemis are goal-oriented. They enjoy "the chase" of elusive quarry. Their perseverance leads to accomplishment and achievement. Artemis rescued anyone (especially women) in physical danger who appealed for her help. Artemis was the goddess of childbirth. The Romans knew Artemis as Diana.

Emotional Control System
Artemis energy is about seeking and anticipation—the goal-directed search for food, shelter, mates, etc.

Life Purpose

An Artemis woman's life purpose is to achieve goals.

Shadow

Too much Artemis energy results in endless searching, to the point of exhaustion. Or an Artemis woman can be "so focused on her own aims and undistracted that she fails to notice the feelings of others around her."[360]

Artemis's shadow includes contempt for vulnerability, and difficulties with intimacy. She was associated with goal-directed, merciless, destructive rage:

> Outrage at wrongs done, loyalty to others, strength to express a point of view, and a propensity to take action can be very positive characteristics of Artemis and Artemis women. But the mercilessness of the punishment they mete out can be appalling. [E.g., 1970s feminists raged at men] with intense hostility that was often out of proportion to the particular provocation.[361]
> — Jean Shinoda Bolen, *Goddesses in Everywoman* (1984)

Under Stress

Under stress, Artemis becomes her brother Apollo. Artemis women think clearly and unemotionally under pressure.

When Safe

When safe, Artemis becomes Demeter. When they can, Artemis women help less-fortunate individuals.

Other Personality Type Systems

Artemis isn't represented in astrology. Artemis is Enneagram personality type #8, the Boss.

Sex

Artemis women see sex as an adventure. For them, sex is a recreational sport, not an expression of commitment (Hera) or an occasion for sensuality (Aphrodite).

A lesbian Artemis woman will have many friends, a band of nymphs looking for adventure. If her lover is another Artemis woman (her "identical twin") she should consider whether her partner is her best friend or her romantic lover. She may better off with a more feminine lover—the goddess and her nymph.

Apollo–Artemis Marriage

An Apollo–Artemis marriage tempers goal-seeking (and adventure) with good sense. A couple that successfully uses this energy achieves their goals—and has stories to tell their grandchildren.

Apollo

Apollo men approach marriage as they approach applying to law school. They rationally decide whether a woman will be a good match, rather than acting on passion or impulse.

Artemis

For a relationship with an Artemis woman, a man shouldn't be Orion, the hunter and Ares archetype. Her competitive nature unintentionally caused his death. Challenge her, and she'll obsess until she wins—another man to beat.

> But if he moves closer emotionally, wants to marry her, or becomes dependent on her, the excitement of the "hunt" is over. Moreover, she may lose interest or feel contempt for him if he shows "weakness" by needing her. As a result, an Artemis woman may have a series of relationships that go well only as long as the man keeps some emotional distance and is not always available.[362]
> — Jean Shinoda Bolen, *Goddesses in Everywoman* (1984)

The lasting relationship for an Artemis woman is with an Apollo man. Apollo was her twin brother. Her domain was the wilderness. His was the city. He was the Sun god. She was the Moon goddess. He was the god of domesticated animals. She was the goddess of wild animals. He was the god of laws. She lived in the wilderness, away from civilized laws.

This relationship starts as brother and sister. The Artemis woman may have another boyfriend (or girlfriend). Give her space to roam, and she'll be back at your door when she's "in town."

The story of Atalanta and Hippomenes shows how to marry an Artemis woman.[363] Atalanta was a beautiful princess. She enjoyed hunting and sports. Many men wanted to marry her. She promised to marry the first man to outrun her in a race. Losers were immediately killed. Atalanta won race after race. This is a metaphor that competing with an Artemis woman kills the relationship.

Unathletic Hippomenes (an Apollo man) truly loved her. He decided that death was better than life without her. He prayed to Aphrodite for help. Aphrodite gave him three golden apples.

When Atalanta took off ahead of Hippomenes, he threw the first golden apple into her path. She stopped to pick it up. She saw her face reflected, but distorted by the curving apple. She realized that she would not be young and beautiful forever. Someday her body would sag like the reflection in the apple.

Hippomenes passed her as she pondered this insight. Atalanta took off again, repassing him. He threw the second golden apple. When she stopped to pick it up, Aphrodite caused Atalanta to see in the shiny apple her dead lover, Meleager. She yearned when she remembered their physical and emotional closeness.

Hippomenes passed Atalanta again. She took off and repassed him again. He threw the last golden apple. When she stopped to pick it up, Demeter caused Atalanta to see her reflection, surrounded by loving children. Atalanta was transfixed by the realization that she wanted a family. Hippomenes ran across the finish line. They married that afternoon.

Meeting

To attract an Artemis woman, be civilized, radiantly sunny, and pray to Aphrodite for help.

♥

HERMES–HESTIA

Hermes

"On the freights. He'd worked as general kitchen help in a Los Angeles hotel, but had just been fired when he had 'blown up' and 'told the cook off.' He carried a clean white shirt to look for work. He talked about going to Redding, to Eugene, and to Seattle. He had $1.80." Yuba County, California, April 13, 1940. Photo by Rondal Partridge, National Youth Administration.[364]

Celebrities

Giacomo Casanova, George Custer, Woody Guthrie, Marshall McLuhan, Woody Allen, Ronald Reagan (he only played Zeus), Warren Beatty, Sting, Howard Stern.

Hairstyle

Long enough to suggest wings growing out of his head.

Favorite Television Series

The X-Files, starring David Duchovny, and *The Simpsons*, starring Bart Simpson.

Mythology

Hermes was the trickster. He was a young god who saw nothing wrong with lying and stealing, if it amused him. As the messenger god, he symbolized quick movement, agile thinking, and facile words. He was the god of luck and the unexpected. He was the god of travelers and thieves. He was the only god who could travel to Hades, the realm of the dead. This showed that the depths of the unconscious are accessible only by those who don't take themselves too seriously. The Romans knew Hermes as Mercury.

That the messenger of the gods was a trickster suggests that one should be wary of divine messages.[365]

Emotional Control System

Playing, fun, joy, and humor enable individuals to communicate emotions and forge social bonds. Recreation reduces stress and renews our creative abilities.[366]

Life Purpose

A Hermes man's life purpose is to perceive the world as other people see it, and to help others perceive the world as he sees it. E.g., Ronald Reagan was a successful actor, portraying how various characters perceived their world. He later became the "Great Communicator"—helping Americans see the world as he saw it.

Shadow

As actors, Hermes men can deceive. Often a Hermes man pretends to be a Zeus man—e.g., Ronald Reagan playing the role of President.

Hermes men can't make commitments. They see both sides of every issue—and can't settle on one.

Under Stress

Under stress, Hermes becomes Athena. Put the screws on *The X-Files'* Fox Mulder and he spins out conspiracy theories, with strategies worked out until doomsday.

When Safe

When safe, a Hermes man becomes Hestia. Traveling men sometimes stop and smell the roses.

Other Personality Type Systems

Hermes is represented in astrology by Gemini (seeing two sides of issues, including the humorous side of serious situations), the 3rd House (of Communication), and the planet Mercury. Hermes is Enneagram personality type #7, the Entertainer.

Sex

A Hermes man charms his way into a woman's life—and then disappears as suddenly. He delights women with his here-and-now energy. The relationship goes well if the woman doesn't expect commitment. But beware of Hermes the god of thieves—he can take advantage of a woman who trusts him.

Meeting

To meet Hermes men, get a backpack, a *Lonely Planet* travel guide, and go.

Hestia

Judy Blume, 1978[367]

Celebrities
Women novelists, Martha Stewart's customers, nuns.

Hairstyle
Long but tied up in a scarf.

Shoes
Clogs.

Favorite Movie
Howard's End, starring Emma Thompson (1992).

Mythology
Hestia was the goddess of home, hearth, and garden. The Romans knew Hestia as Vesta.

Emotional Control System
Hestia energy is about "nest-building." Lack of Hestia energy results in feeling homeless, rootless, or impermanent, as if you're living in hotel rooms.

Life Purpose

A Hestia woman's life purpose is to make a beautiful, happy home. Instead of a home, she may make her church beautiful, and make church social groups happy. Or she may be "den mother" of her workplace, the person to whom customers and other employees gravitate as the center of the organization.

Shadow

A Hestia woman's goal is a happy home, not a happy husband or children. If these goals are congruous, all is well. But if the husband's happiness requires a spiritual quest to Tibet, don't expect a Hestia woman to go with him.

A Hestia woman may lack ambitions outside her home. She may even be agoraphobic (unable to leave her home).

Hestia women are *melodramatic*—melancholy plus drama, or creative but unhappy. They're natural novelists. Their inner dramas are more interesting than books, movies, or the real world.

Under Stress

Under stress, Hestia women become Athena. They're ideal planners. They imagine "worst case" scenarios and strategize to prevent these possible futures.

When Safe

When safe, Hestia women become Aphrodite. They become charming and attractive hostesses when entertaining in their beautiful homes.

Other Personality Type Systems

Hestia is represented in astrology by the 4th House (of the Home). Hestia is Enneagram personality type #4, the Artist.

Sex

Sex isn't important to Hestia women. A Hestia woman will accommodate her husband, and may enjoy the "nice, warm experience." She may even easily orgasm. But she won't initiate sex. She's content to go without sex for long periods.

Meeting

To meet Hestia women, go to a gardening or cat show. Don't expect these women to dress in dazzling fashions, or do anything else to attract men. Charm her with your wit, and steal her heart.

Hermes–Hestia Marriage

A Poseidon cowboy may want a Hestia "little woman" to take care of his ranch house. He'll use her and maybe abuse her. He won't respect her. Her lack of interest in his doings outside their home won't stop him from getting into trouble, and possibly losing their home.

The ideal husband for a Hestia woman is a "traveling salesman" Hermes man. His quick wit and energy make their home feel alive. When he's not home, a Hestia woman doesn't think about him or care what he's doing.

> In Greek households, the "herm"—a pillar symbolizing Hermes—stood just outside the front door, and inside a round hearth with a fire in the center represented Hestia.[368]
>
> — Jean Shinoda Bolen, *Gods in Everyman* (1989)

A Hermes–Hestia marriages channels joy and playfulness into a home. A couple that successfully uses this energy makes a happy home—a place they can retreat to when tired, which restores them to go out into the world again. A Hermes father enjoys childcare if he gets to entertain the children.[369]

ARES–HEPHAESTUS–APHRODITE

Ares

"Cpl. Carlton Chapman is a machine-gunner in an M-4 tank, attached to a Motor Transport unit." Nancy, France, November 5, 1944. Photo by Ryan, Office of the Chief Signal Officer.[370]

Celebrities

Muhammad Ali, Mikhail Baryshinikov, Michael Jordan, Sean Penn.

Hairstyle

A razor has never come upon my head....If I be shaved, then my strength will leave me, and I shall become weak, and be like any other man.

— Samson, *Judges 16:17*

Shoes
Heavy boots.

Favorite Movie
Rambo, starring Sylvester Stallone (1986).

Mythology
Ares was the lover and the warrior. His tutor Priapus (a fertility god renowned for his huge penis) first trained Ares to be a dancer, and later trained him to be a warrior.

> **You don't give a man a weapon until you've taught him how to dance.**[371]
>
> — **Celtic proverb**

The Romans knew Ares as Mars.

Emotional Control System
Anger and rage, when confined, thwarted, or frustrated.

Life Purpose
Ares's life purpose is independence. Ares men use courage and initiative to gain freedom. Ares men can be leaders, or work independently. They're never followers or subordinates.

Shadow
Ares men can't stand being controlled, especially by anonymous strangers. They'll sacrifice their best interests for freedom. E.g., they'll take a cut in pay to work independently rather than work for a big corporation.

They underestimate things in their path—other people, time requirements, mountains.

They challenge people. They use "anger as a greeting," but respect individuals who stand up to them.

They always feel they're right, but don't hesitate to change their views when they receive new information.

Under Stress

Under stress, Ares becomes Apollo. Watch Muhammad Ali's 1973 fight against George Foreman, in the movie *When We Were Kings*. Ali came into the ring with a plan, and coolly kept to his plan even as Foreman pummeled Ali in the initial rounds.

When Safe

When safe, Ares men become Demeter. They can be generous and supportive to a child or employee. Justice concerns them. They support underdogs.

Other Personality Type Systems

Ares is represented in astrology by Aries (courage, initiative, independence, and the will to exist), the 1st House (of the Self, or establishing one's identity), and the planet Mars. Ares is Enneagram personality type #8, the Boss.

Sex

Ares was Aphrodite's favorite lover.

Meeting

To meet Ares men, wear red and go to sporting events.

Hephaestus

Robert Oppenheimer (left) and General Leslie Groves standing over remains of first atomic bomb, detonated July 16, 1945, near Alamogordo, New Mexico.[372]

Celebrities
Thomas Edison, Albert Einstein, Robert Oppenheimer, James Doohan (Scotty) on *Star Trek*, Bill Gates.

Hairstyle
Short, but can't talk about sports with Frank the barber.

Shoes
Rockports—inside white anti-radiation booties.

Favorite Movie
Star Trek: First Contact, starring James Cromwell as Dr. Zefram Cochrane (1996).

Mythology
Hephaestus was the craftsman, the god of the forge. He built tools,

weapons, chariots and everything else the other gods used. The Romans knew Hephaestus as Vulcan.

Hephaestus had a clubfoot. The other gods rejected him because of his disability. He lived alone in a volcano. As god of volcanoes he had immense destructive power.

Emotional Control System

Speculatively, the use of tools and the control of fire may be hardwired into our brains.

Life Purpose

A Hephaestus man's life purpose is to develop skills and competence. He wants to make useful things.

Shadow

Hephaestus men are nerdy—good with machines or computers, but not with people. They can be insensitive about their powerful creations hurting people. E.g., Robert Oppenheimer and the atomic bomb, or Bill Gates building his empire.

Under Stress

Under stress, Hephaestus becomes Apollo. Take him to a weird party, and he'll act like an anthropologist visiting an exotic tribe—observing, occasionally talking to people, but staying detached and emotionally uninvolved.

When Safe

When safe, a Hephaestus man becomes Demeter. He offers his skills to help other people.

Other Personality Type Systems

Hephaestus is represented in astrology by Virgo (developing skills and competence), and the 6th House (of Servants). Hephaestus is Enneagram personality type #8, the Boss.

Sex

Engineers use "elegant" and "beautiful" to describe well-built things. Engineers talking about computer code sound like women talking about cocktail dresses.

Meeting

To meet Hephaestus men, go to a computer conference or Star Trek convention. Look for the men with no social skills and multitudinous stock options. Show off your golden hair, and ask him to fix your computer. When he finishes, your computer will do stuff that you never imagined, or wanted to do.

Aphrodite

Celebrities

Georgia O'Keefe, Lauren Bacall, Elizabeth Taylor, Princess Diana, Madonna.

Marilyn Monroe, 1955[373]

Hairstyle

Long and wild. Hair that men want to feel brush against their naked chests.[374] E.g., Cindy Crawford, Claudia Schiffer.

Shoes
High heels, platforms.

Favorite Movie
Gentlemen Prefer Blondes, starring Marilyn Monroe (1953).

Mythology
Aphrodite was the goddess of feminine love and beauty. She had the power to cause mortals and deities to fall in love. The Romans knew Aphrodite as Venus.

Emotional Control System
Aphrodite is a combination of two emotional control systems: sexuality and homeostasis.

No one has ever referred to Aphrodite as the "goddess of homeostasis." But this is the nature of pleasure: when our bodies are out of balance, we suffer. When we get, do, or consume what we need to return to homeostasis, we feel pleasure. E.g., when you're cold, nothing is so pleasurable as a hot drink.

When an Aphrodite woman's body signals that it's out of balance, she looks for an opportunity to experience the pleasure of returning to homeostasis. E.g., jumping into a cool creek on a hot day. Her pains and pleasures are immediate, not some time in the future.

Sexuality is a different emotional control system.[375]

Life Purpose
The goddess of homeostasis's life purpose is to seek physical comforts.

The goddess of love's life purpose is to be charming and attractive.

Shadow
The shadow side of the goddess of homeostasis is addictions.

Neurologically, addictions are messed up homeostatic systems.

The goddess of love's shadow side is shallow, uncommitted relationships. An Aphrodite woman may sleep around. Or she may be like Elizabeth Taylor, who married eight times.

Actresses who use Aphrodite sexiness—e.g., Bo Derek, Brigitte Nielsen (married five times, including to Sylvester Stallone)—quickly rise to movie star status. Then their careers fall just as fast. The public seems to want only a "one-night stand" with Aphrodite actresses.[376]

Under Stress

Under stress, Aphrodite becomes Athena. Invite an Aphrodite woman camping. She'll come up with a list of fears, from snakes to not being able to wash her hair.

When Safe

When safe, Aphrodite becomes Hestia. She'll make her home and garden as beautiful as herself.

Other Personality Type Systems

Aphrodite is represented in astrology by Leo (outward expression, seeking attention), the 5th House (of Children, and recreation), and the planet Venus. Aphrodite is Enneagram personality type #7, the Entertainer.

Sex

Expect great sex with an Aphrodite woman—while the relationship lasts.

Meeting

To meet Aphrodite women, embody Ares. Aphrodite women are everywhere, looking beautiful and attracting men. To win one, show courage. Not money or status, but the confidence and will to win her.

Keep her by embodying Hephaestus. If you're a software engineer during the week and a motorcycle racer on weekends, attract her with your motorcycle. Keep her by fixing her computer.

Ares–Hephaestus–Aphrodite Marriage

An Ares–Hephaestus–Aphrodite marriage works hard and plays hard. On weekdays, Hephaestus and Aphrodite get the work done that's necessary for homeostasis (e.g., food, shelter, clothing). At night and on weekends, Ares and Aphrodite have passionate romance and great sex.

Ares

An Ares man can be good husband, if his wife doesn't try to control him. He can be a good citizen in a community that looks to him as a leader.

Hephaestus

Hephaestus men live for women. They need women to appreciate the beautiful things they make. They need women to inspire their creativity, to teach them social skills, and to tell the world that they're brilliant.

Hephaestus men are the best husbands. They never argue. Any problem is an opportunity to invent something to fix the problem.

Hephaestus men are faithful to their wives, usually because no other woman wants them. But Hephaestus men can neglect their wives, spending too much time at work. A Hephaestus man's wife may not get the passion and fireworks that she wants, but this doesn't mean that he doesn't treasure his wife more than anything in the world.

Hephaestus built golden maidservants that could talk and perform household tasks. A Hephaestus man might buy a Russian mail-order bride, expecting a golden maidservant. He's more likely to get Pandora, the first mortal woman, whom Hephaestus also built. Pandora had not only domestic skills and sex appeal, but also "shamelessness, cunning use of language, lies, and deceitfulness."[377]

Aphrodite

Aphrodite women shouldn't marry Hermes men. They'll have fun for a while, but the marriage will lack commitment. Avoid Poseidon men, unless you think Courtney Love enjoyed scraping Kurt Cobain's brains off the wall.

Just as Aphrodite is a combination of two goddesses, her marriage involves two gods. Aphrodite married Hephaestus, god of the forge. Aphrodite women love the beautiful things Hephaestus men make for their wives.

But Aphrodite's lover was Ares, god of war. They shared intensity, sensuality, immediacy, and passion.

Ares men often have Hephaestus jobs (jobs that use tools), e.g., auto mechanics. Many Hephaestus computer nerds become Ares weekend warriors, enjoying flying, mountain biking, etc.

Marital success for an Aphrodite woman requires bringing out the Hephaestus in her Ares man, or the Ares in her Hephaestus man. Aphrodite and Ares had two sons, Fear and Panic. If you don't want TV crews asking why your sons blew up their high school, have your Ares husband channel your sons' energy into Hephaestus skills (e.g., building a really cool car for Mom).

To bring out the Ares in your Hephaestus nerd, suggest that he buy a motorcycle. Don't ride on the back until he passes the Motorcycle Safety Foundation course, and buys you a helmet, leather jacket, and cool new boots. Then suggest a drive up to the city for spicy Thai food, and return on Skyline with a starry stop at a scenic overlook.

Suggest watching a swing dance video. Watch it in his living room. Don't take him dancing in public yet. You'll embarrass him. He'll need a lot of practice before he's ready to lead you on a dance floor. But when he figures out that *leading* means that you'll do whatever swings and spins he wants you to do, watch Ares come out. Combined with Hephaestus's 900 megahertz learning skills, once he's interested in swing dance he won't stop until he's mastered every move.

DIONYSUS–DEMETER

Dionysus

Bhagwan Shree Rajneesh (Osho)
© Osho International www.osho.com

Celebrities

Viktor Frankl, John Lennon,
Jerry Garcia, Charles Manson,
Roger Daltrey, Robert Plant,
James Taylor, John Belushi,
Bhagwan Shree Rajneesh
(Osho).

Hairstyle
Long, wild, sexy hair and beard.

Shoes
Sandals.

Mythology
Dionysus was the god of wine. He was also the god of ecstasy and enraptured love, pain and suffering, and death and rebirth. He traveled widely, teaching grape cultivation and winemaking. Madness and violence followed him. Women worshipped him. The women drank wine, danced wildly, then tore an animal to pieces and ate the raw flesh. The Romans knew him as Bacchus.

Emotional Control System
The *quest for meaning* may be hardwired into our brains.

Life Purpose
A Dionysus man's life purpose is a quest for meaning. He lives by

192

ideals and principles that he has yet to discover.

Shadow

Dionysus men lack "real world" goals. They're questing for principles, and haven't yet discovered these principles.

They enjoy resting or doing nothing—especially if alcoholic beverages are available. When faced with a decision they let their partner decide, saying, "I'll be happy with whatever makes you happy."

A Dionysus man has a close relationship with his mother. He is her "divine child," with a sense of specialness or destiny. In adult life, a Dionysus man may resent people not recognizing his specialness, e.g., when they expect him to do mundane work. He may have mood swings between low self-esteem and ego inflation. He may have substance abuse issues.

"Wounding" is central to Dionysus. "Wounding" can be a life-threatening illness, e.g., cancer, which makes a man feel as if he has been dismembered and then reassembled as a new person.[379] Or "wounding" can be a painful experience that forces an individual to break from "the flat ennui of numbing conformity to cultural and familial expectations."[380] E.g., Vietnam veterans say that their experiences hurt them deeply and forced them to question their

Women worshipping Bhagwan Shree Rajneesh, Oregon, 1981. Photo by Bill Miller.[378]

government and the previous generation's values, but the hard lessons were worth learning.

Dionysus men can become cult leaders. They attract followers, especially women. But the followers go mad. The followers may commit crimes opposite to the ideals espoused by their leader. E.g., no evidence indicated that Bhagwan Shree Rajneesh was involved in his followers' poisoning of 751 residents of The Dalles, Oregon (see "Women's Power," page 40).

Under Stress

Under stress, Dionysus individuals become Poseidon. They become wildly, out-of-control emotional.

When Safe

Under safety, Dionysus becomes Zeus. E.g., when Bhagwan Shree Rajneesh became rich he wanted to be respectable. He wanted Rolls-Royce automobiles. Unable to control himself, he bought 93 Rolls-Royces.

Other Personality Type Systems

Dionysus is represented in astrology by Sagittarius (the quest for meaning), and the 9th House (of Long Journeys Over Water, and higher education). Dionysus is Enneagram personality type #9, the Peacemaker.

Sex

Women surround Dionysus men. A Dionysus man has many female friends, and many of these are lovers. His emotional wounds attract their nurturing instinct. His sensuality and appreciation of their beauty, and his ecstatic lovemaking becomes addictive to women. Dionysus is

> ...the more feminized male ideal, who started rearing his long-haired head in the late 1960s and early '70s. Though they carried themselves with all-male swagger, frontmen Roger Daltrey of The Who and Robert Plant of Led Zeppelin were clearly in touch with their feminine sides.

Women couldn't get enough of these emotional yet masculine men....1980s hair bands such as Mötley Crüe and Poison [showed that] some women liked men all dolled up in makeup and hairspray wearing pants that left absolutely nothing to the imagination.[381]

— Kate Flatley

Meeting

To meet Dionysus men, go to a wine bar—or join a cult.

Demeter

"Nipomo, Calif. Mar. 1936. Migrant agricultural worker's family. Seven hungry children. Mother aged 32. Destitute in a pea pickers camp, because of the failure of the early pea crop. These people had just sold their tent in order to buy food. Most of the 2,500 people in this camp were destitute." Photo by Dorothea Lange, Farm Security Administration.[382]

Celebrities

Eleanor Roosevelt, Mother Theresa, Barbara Bush.

Favorite Movie
Little Women, starring Susan Sarandon, Claire Danes, and Winona Ryder (1994).

Mythology
Demeter was the goddess of the harvest and of motherhood. The Romans knew Demeter as Ceres (the root of our word *cereal*).

Emotional Control System
Demeter energy is *nurturing*.

Life Purpose
A Demeter woman lives for her children, or to help other people. Demeter women love their children regardless of whether a child is rebellious, disabled, gay, or governor of Texas.

Shadow
Demeter women *give to get love*. They'll sacrifice their own needs, then expect something back. They give unsolicited help, then feel used or cheated when the recipient doesn't express gratitude or return a favor. The problem isn't ungrateful recipients. The problem is that the Demeter woman doesn't recognize that people don't need her help.

Too much Demeter energy makes an individual obsessed with diet, stress-reduction classes, or fitness. Too little Demeter energy leads to working long hours without eating, relaxing, or taking a vacation. A woman who works too much may overcompensate by obsession with diet and fitness.

Under Stress
Under stress, Demeter women become Artemis, Ares, and Hephaestus. After Hades abducted Demeter's daughter, Demeter wandered over the earth, day and night, without eating or drinking.[383] This is the *seeking behavior* emotional control system, symbolized by Artemis.

Everywhere Demeter wandered, she broke plows, destroyed

farms and cattle, made fields barren, and blighted seeds so they couldn't grow.[384] She used her *anger* emotional control system, symbolized by Ares.

Finally, Demeter disguised herself as an old woman. She met the daughters of the king of Eleusis (near Athens). She offered to do any domestic work in their household.[385] Willingness to work is symbolized by Hephaestus.

When Safe

When safe, Demeter women become Apollo. They enjoy a symphony or art museum.

Other Personality Type Systems

Demeter is represented in astrology by Cancer (empathy and nurturing). Demeter is Enneagram personality type #2, the Nurturer.

Sex

Demeter women are warm and affectionate, but are more into hugs than sex. Use condoms because she may not be using birth control. If she gets pregnant, she'll keep the child.

Meeting

To meet Demeter women, play with children. Borrow a baby and go to a beach. Go to a park and play with women's dogs.

Dionysus–Demeter Marriage

A Dionysus–Demeter marriage tempers wounding and nurturing. A couple that successfully uses this energy heals their psychological and spiritual traumas.

Dionysus

Dionysus's marriage to Ariadne was the only healthy marriage on Mt. Olympus.[386] (Anyone who wants "a marriage made in heaven" hasn't read Greek mythology.)

But the wife of a Dionysus man can also find her life alternating between ecstasy and suffering, between "pandemonium and deathly silence."[387]

Demeter

Demeter women marry for children. The husband—or sperm donor—is only a means to her end.

Zeus men are happy to provide sperm, but their relationship goes downhill—fast—after the transfer.

A Dionysus–Demeter marriage echoes Mary and Jesus. His central issue was "wounding" and suffering. Her central ability was nurturing. A Dionysus–Demeter marriage may look like a mother/son relationship, but they'll give what the other needs.

HADES–PERSEPHONE

Hades

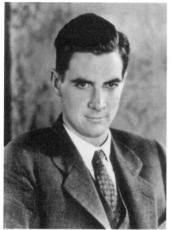

Howard Hughes, 1936
© MPTV.NET

Celebrities

Sigmund Freud, Howard Hughes, Vincent Price, Christopher Reeve, vampires, serial killers, drummers in rock bands,[388] male hairdressers.

Favorite Movie

The Sixth Sense, starring Bruce Willis (1999).

Mythology

Hades ruled the underworld, the realm of the dead. He was wealthy beyond counting, but was a recluse. Hades wore a cap of invisibility when he left the underworld. The Romans knew Hades as Pluto.

Emotional Control Systems

Hades symbolizes the psychic pain of sorrow, grief, and loneliness—and the psychological insights this can lead us to.

Shadow

A Hades man may make people connect to deep feelings, but not help them move to higher states of consciousness. E.g., O.J. Simpson made millions of Americans aware of deep, hidden racist feelings, but he didn't do anything to improve relations between the races.

Other Personality Type Systems

Hades is represented in astrology by Scorpio (basing one's life on one's deepest convictions), and the 8th House (of Death, and major transformation). Hades isn't represented in the Enneagram.

Sex and Marriage

If you liked *Interview with the Vampire*, by Anne Rice (1976) you'll love Hades men.

But Hades men can be invisible to women. A Hades man may not be good at flirting or dating. He may have elaborate, deep fantasies rather than relationships with real women. If he tries to make a relationship real, the woman may accuse him of abduction—perhaps only because he lacks social skills.

Hades men can deeply love women, in committed, faithful relationships. Marriage can draw a Hades man out of reclusion, and into participation in family and community.

Meeting

To meet Hades men, wear Goth black velvet dresses. Dive into the depths of depression, and look around at who's there.

Persephone

Sylvia Plath, 1959[389]

Celebrities

Ophelia in *Hamlet*; Laura in Tennessee Williams' *The Glass Menagerie* (1944); Sylvia Plath; Dory Previn (*Mythical Kings and Iguanas* singer-songwriter, André Previn's wife); Hannah Green, author of *I Never Promised You a Rose Garden* (1988).

Hairstyle

Changes her hairstyle to reflect personal growth. Tries new hairstyles to try new directions for personal growth.[390]

Shoes
Platform Mary Janes.

Favorite Movie
The Cell, starring Jennifer Lopez (2000).

Mythology
Persephone was the young daughter of Zeus and Demeter. She was picking flowers one day. When she pulled an especially beautiful narcissus, the earth split open. Hades, ruler of the dead, thundered up in his golden chariot pulled by four black horses. He grabbed the screaming maiden and carried her down to the underworld.

As Demeter searched for her daughter, her despair caused crops to die. Humans starved in the cold, bleak, endless winter. They could no longer sacrifice to the gods. Because the gods wanted humans to worship them, they pressured Zeus to send Hermes to return Persephone to her mother.

The Fates decreed that Persephone could return only if she'd eaten nothing in the underworld. Persephone had eaten nothing in her depression, but then Hades gave her a pomegranate. A pomegranate is a refreshing, delicious fruit with many seeds that look like rubies. Persephone, like most girls, couldn't resist plucking at enticing foods. She ate a few seeds of the pomegranate. Then Hermes arrived to fetch her. When Demeter asked Persephone if she'd eaten anything in the underworld, Persephone lied that Hades tricked her into eating the pomegranate. Because she'd voluntarily eaten the fruit, the gods obliged her to spend part of the year in the underworld and part of the year with her mother.

As Queen of the Underworld, Persephone guided mortals who descended to the realm of the dead on a quest. When the musician Orpheus came looking for his dead wife, his song was so beautiful that Persephone granted his wish and restored his wife's life. When Aphrodite sent Psyche to the underworld for cosmetics, Persephone filled Aphrodite's box (the word *psychology* derives from Psyche's name). When Heracles (a.k.a. Hercules) descended to Hades for his 12th labor, Persephone helped the hero bring

Hades' three-headed dog Cerberus to show the king of Mycenae.

The Romans called her Proserpina. Persephone as the innocent maiden was Kore (the Romans called her Cora), to distinguish her from Persephone as Queen of the Underworld.

Emotional Control System

Persephone symbolizes separation distress, from one's mother or, more broadly, from one's old life to a new life. Separation distress is the basis of anxiety and panic attacks.

Life Purpose

A Persephone woman's life purpose is to separate from her past, and transform into a new person. She then guides other individuals through personal transformations. Ideal professions include counseling psychology or social work.

A Persephone psychologist sees depression and mental illness not as symptoms to be medicated or eradicated, but as profound journeys. The sojourner goes through pain and suffering, but sooner or later reaches a greater level of consciousness. Just as Persephone guided Odysseus, Heracles, Psyche, and Orpheus in their journeys to the underworld, a Persephone psychologist guides a patient to find what his life's treasure, and then return to the world of the living. Hades, which was the name of both the underworld and its king, had uncountable riches. This symbolized that personal growth can lead to great rewards. Persephone psychologists are usually transpersonal or Jungian psychologists.

Shadow

Persephone women are passive, compliant and uncommitted to goals. Our culture views these qualities as undesirable. But sometimes it's better to not act decisively, and instead wait patiently until a situation changes for the better.

A Persephone woman may escape into a fantasy world. She may be psychically gifted. She may suffer from psychiatric illness or anorexia. Depression makes her "fade away" quietly, as opposed to forcing her depression onto others (as Demeter did).

A Persephone woman tries to please her mother and be a "good girl." She expects teachers or supervisors to hold her hand through each step. But Persephone lied to her mother about the pomegranate. A Persephone woman will use deviousness, lying, and manipulation, while maintaining the image of innocence.

Other Personality Type Systems

Persephone is represented in astrology by Pisces (lifting the veil of the universe), and the 12th House (of Troubles, and finding peaceful sanctuary, e.g., prayer, at the center of bad things happening to good people). Persephone isn't represented in the Enneagram.

Sex

Buy her *Screw the Roses, Send Me the Thorns: The Romance and Sexual Sorcery of Sadomasochism*, by Philip Miller and Molly Devon (1995). She'll say, "I've never told anyone this, but all my life I've fantasized about bondage. How did you know?"

An advice columnist received the following letter:

> My friend is the most wonderful, caring, loving person I've ever met, but also the most naïve. I know from personal experience that she has an unusually large sexual appetite, little if any interest in foreplay, and cannot seem to reach orgasm, ever. I am sure that I'm not her only current partner, as much as she assures me I am. In the past, she has given herself away so many times, I can't count them. For all her goodness, I've seen her lie to other people so convincingly they wouldn't believe she was lying, even if you told them. My concern now is not me, but her....Even if I never touched her again, I really do care about her and would like to help her.[391]

Meeting

To meet Persephone women, care about other individuals, act decisively, and wear a black cape.

Hades–Persephone Marriage

A Hades–Persephone marriage is transformational. A couple that successfully uses this energy guides each other through life-changing experiences. They separate (possibly painfully) from the past. They mature to higher stages of personal growth.

Caring About More People

Humans, more than other animals, depend on social organization for survival. Individuals, today or 100,000 years ago, with more relationships survive and prosper.

As our ancestors evolved, they lived in larger groups (see "Cities and Civilization," page 35). Larger brains enabled them to keep track of more relationships (and may have contributed to the evolution of larger brains).

As our individual development mirrors our ancestors' evolution (see "Ontogeny Recapitulates Phylogeny," page 3), we care about more people as we mature. We begin life concerned only about our own needs. A young adult cares about his or her romantic partner. A mature adult cares about his or her family. A clan elder cares about the survival of the clan. Personal growth is, stage by stage, caring about increasing numbers of people.

Caring about other people entails personal suffering. Our minds produce psychic pain (pain that originates in the mind) to push us to accept physical pain. Psychic pain can be stronger than physical pain. E.g., a hunter brings home only a rabbit. He has to decide between feeding his family and feeling hunger, or feeding himself and feeling guilt.

Skipping Life Stages

Personal growth wasn't an issue before the current era. Puberty made young people want a partner. Procreation led to caring about a family. Arranging children's marriages led to caring about other families. Environmental crises forced individuals into leadership roles for the survival of the clan.

The modern world isn't so straightforward. Adolescents sexually mature earlier, due to better nutrition. We marry later, because our society demands more education.

Our ancestors were most aware of suffering around them. In contrast, our "electronic global village" makes us aware of suffering in far-off corners of the globe. We "think globally" as soon as we're old enough to watch television news. Yet we care less about the people we're closest to.

Our minds are hardwired to jump ahead to our next stage of personal growth. Traditional societies don't facilitate jumping ahead, but our society does. If a welfare program pays teenage girls to produce babies, the girls skip the marriage stage and jump to the motherhood stage. If television news enables us to care about people on the other side of the world, we jump to *agape* and skip developing a loving relationship with one partner.

Lack of Emotional Range

Our ancestors endured great suffering, e.g., extremes of weather, or long periods with little food. Human brains evolved to balance suffering and happiness. The greatest joy follows the greatest suffering (see "Emotional Range," page 115).

The modern world minimizes physical suffering, yet our brains continue to balance happiness and suffering. Our narrower emotional range leads us to differentiate finer levels of happiness and suffering, e.g., driving a Lexus vs. a Chevy. We confuse personal growth with appreciating luxury goods.

To avoid such confusion, seek extremes of suffering and joy. Run marathons. Travel to third-world countries. Forget about job security and instead do what you love, even if you have to drive a Chevy.

Getting Stuck

Sometimes we feel stuck between stages of personal growth. We don't get stuck because we lack a vision of our new life. We all have dreams of a better life.

We don't get stuck because we don't know how to get to our new life. We don't know every step on the way, but we all know at least one step we could take.

We get stuck because we avoid the suffering of the transition to our new life. E.g., quitting your job to do what you love might require trading in your Lexus for a Chevy.

Most individuals are more or less equally happy. CEOs and janitors report feeling happy the same number of hours per day, and report the same number of hours of unhappiness. Only individuals with many relationships are more often happy than other individuals. I.e., only loneliness can make us unhappy more than we're happy. Connection to a partner, family, and community is the only way to be happy more than you're unhappy.

Psychic Pain Indicates Readiness for Personal Growth

The modern world eliminates physical suffering. We now feel psychic pain with no connection to physical suffering.

The modern world confuses our stages of personal growth. We now feel psychic pain with no indication of the direction in which we need to grow.

Psychic pain—e.g., depression, anxiety, guilt—indicates that we're ready to mature to a new stage of personal growth.

One response is to numb psychic pain. E.g., alcohol, Prozac, "feel good" psychology, or switching on a television. Another response is to buy luxury goods. But your psychic pain soon returns, making you repeat the process.

Self-destructive behavior is a third response. Everything that reminds you of your old self—e.g., spouse, job, neighborhood, hobbies—causes psychic pain. You try to destroy your old life, instead of building a new life.

The Hades–Persephone Relationship

(Men and women can use either Hades or Persephone behavior. To simplify language, I use male pronouns to refer to Hades partners, and female pronouns to refer to Persephone partners.)

In a Hades–Persephone relationship, the Hades partner forces the Persephone partner to change. He loves her without loving her present or past self. He sees her emerging new life stage and loves her for that, but without projecting his own issues onto her.

He forces her to experience pain and suffering. He maintains a close, supportive relationship until she's through her painful transformation.

The Hades partner must do two, contradictory actions:

• Care about his partner more than cares about himself.

• Do not what he's told, but what must be done.

E.g., a favorite theme of movies is an individual putting himself in harm's way to help another individual, while at the same time rejecting orders from an authority figure. A hero takes decisive action, and takes responsibility for his action.

Caring about another person more than yourself is a feminine trait. Doing not what you're told, but what must be done is a masculine trait. Combined, the Hades partner uses masculine and feminine behaviors at the same time. He transcends gender roles. The relationship transforms him, as well as transforming his partner.

The wrong masculine response is to selfishly do what you want to do, ignoring what you're told, caring only about your own needs. The wrong feminine response is to do what another person requests, against the other person's best interests, or against your own best interests (i.e., self-sacrificing behavior).

A Hades–Persephone relationship demands deep, immediate commitment. Such a relationship takes place right here, right now. You're committing to the relationship until your partner reaches the next stage of her personal growth. This could be years, or could be hours. Don't be afraid to enter a Hades–Persephone relationship —you're not committing to a lifetime together.

A Hades–Persephone relationship is a moral dilemma for the Hades partner. If he does what she tells him to do, he fails to care about her. If he does what must be done, he's acting against her will (and possibly against the law).

Why Women Do Things to Drive the Men They Love Up the Wall

A woman uses Persephone behavior to test whether her man is capable of being Hades. She uses Persephone behavior—passive-aggressive, self-destructive, or just annoying—to communicate that she's unhappy with her present life and wants to move to a new stage of personal growth. She tests whether he loves her for who she will be—her inner, emerging self—not who she is now.

With a Dionysus partner (e.g., a cult leader), a Persephone woman gets madness. With an Ares partner, she gets physical abuse. With a Poseidon partner, she gets emotional abuse. With Zeus, she gets cheated on. Hermes and Apollo talk with her endlessly (with and without jokes, respectively). With Hephaestus, she gets useful electronic gadgets.

But with a Hades partner, a Persephone woman goes through pain and suffering with her partner's attention and support. She's transformed to a new stage of personal growth.

Hades and Persephone in Every Marriage

Artemis, Athena, and Hestia women don't need men. A Hera woman needs a husband, but he can be absent or even dead. A Demeter woman needs only a sperm donor. Aphrodite women enjoy men, but are happy with fun, shallow relationships.

Persephone women exasperate men, but they're the only women who need intimacy with men. A Persephone woman needs a strong, loving man to support her through painful but necessary transformation. Persephone women are "high maintenance" but worth it.

Looked at another way, all women have all seven goddesses in them. When they're using the other six archetypes they have little or no need for men. But a woman goes into Persephone mode to express her need for intimacy with her man. When your woman becomes a self-destructive "lunachick" and drives you up the wall, she's not trying to break off the relationship. She's trying to transform herself, yourself, and the relationship to next level.

RECOMMENDED BOOKS

Order the following books—at substantial discounts—from
http://www.FriendshipCenter.com/hearts/

The Evolution of the Human Brain

The Biology of Transcendence: A Blueprint of the Human Spirit, by Joseph Chilton Pearce (2002), begins with an excellent 70-page presentation of the triune brain.

"Natural vs. Sexual Selection" is largely from *The Mating Mind: How Sexual Choice Shaped the Evolution of Human Nature*, by Geoffrey F. Miller (2000).

QUOTATIONS AND MENTIONS
Fari Amini, and Richard Lannon

A General Theory of Love, by Thomas Lewis, Fari Amini, and Richard Lannon (2000), page 2.

The Origin of Species, by Charles Darwin (1859), page 3.

The Descent of Man, by Charles Darwin (1871), pages 4 and 4.

How Women Select Men

"How Women Select Men" and "How Men Select Women" are largely from *Evolutionary Psychology: The New Science of the Mind*, by David M. Buss (1999). It's a college textbook but not dry or boring. The writing is clear and easier to read than the "bestsellers." Topics include human survival in nature, men's and women's mating strategies, parenting and kinship, altruism, cooperation, aggression, conflict, and social dominance.

For more about emotions, start with *Emotional Intelligence*, by Daniel Goleman (1994). You'll learn how to improve your ability to use a range of emotions. You'll also learn to appreciate different emotional styles in other people. Then read *The Relationship Cure*, by John Gottman (2001), to improve your skills at recognizing and responding to emotional messages; and *The Emotional Revolution*, by Norman E. Rosenthal (2002), for the latest neuroscientific discoveries and treatments of emotional disorders, including depression, anxiety, and anger.

QUOTATIONS AND MENTIONS

The Biology of Transcendence, by Joseph Chilton Pearce (2002), pages 14 and 15.

The Psychology of Personal Constructs, by George Kelly (1955), page 16.

One Thousand and One Arabian Nights, page 20.

The Mating Mind, by Geoffrey Miller (2000), page 22.

How Men Select Women

QUOTATIONS AND MENTIONS

The Picture of Dorian Gray, by Oscar Wilde (1890), page 23.

How Our Ancestors Lived

This chapter is largely from *Women in Prehistory*, by Margaret Ehrenberg (1989). The book focuses on women and their relationships with men in Paleolithic (hunter-gatherer) and Neolithic (early agricultural) societies.

I also recommend *Humans: An Introduction To Four-Field Anthropology*, by Alice B. Kehoe (1998). This easy-to-read textbook covers the evolution of primates and humans; the Paleolithic, Neolithic, and beginnings of civilization; linguistics; cultural ecology; economics; social organization; and religion.

I don't recommend *The Chalice and the Blade*, by Riane Eisler (1988). For a critique of Eisler's "gynocentric" hypothesis, read *The Myth of Matriarchal Prehistory: Why an Invented Past Won't Give Women a Future*, by Cynthia Eller (2000).

QUOTATIONS AND MENTIONS

Germania, by Tacitus (circa A.D. 100), pages 30, 31, and 41.

Parlor Politics, by Catherine Allgor (2000), page 36.

Monogamy and Polygamy

Women of Principle: Female Networking in Contemporary Mormon Polygyny, by Janet Bennion (1998), quoted on pages 39, 40, and 41, is a fascinating study of women in a Montana polygynist community.

The section about Christian polygyny was from *After Polygamy Was Made a Sin: The Social History of Christian Polygamy*, by John Cairncross (1974).

Sex in America: A Definitive Survey, by Robert Michael, John Gagnon, Edward Laumann, and Gina Bari Kolata (1994), presents the only statistically accurate survey of intimate relationships. The survey included how couples met, how many partners individuals had, sexual practices, and risk factors for STDs. The surprises were not in what Americans do—the large majority of Americans are in traditional relationships—but in the contrast between media messages (e.g., *Sex and the City*) and reality.

QUOTATIONS AND MENTIONS

The Descent of Man, by Charles Darwin (1871), page 39.

Polygamous Families in Contemporary Society, by Irwin Altman and Joseph Ginat (1996), page 42.

Polygamy Reconsidered, by Father Eugene Hillman (1975), page 45.

The Tipping Point, by Malcolm Gladwell (2000), page 48.

Hormones

This chapter is from An Introduction to Behavioral Endocrinology, by Randy Nelson (2000), Sexual Pharmacology: Drugs That Affect Sexual Function, by Theresa Crenshaw and James Goldberg (1996), and *Queer Science: The Use and Abuse of Research on Homosexuality*, by Simon Le Vay (1996).

Communication Styles

This chapter is largely from *You Just Don't Understand: Women and Men in Conversation*, by Deborah Tannen (1990).

QUOTATIONS AND MENTIONS

The Gift of Fear, by Gavin De Becker (1997), page 71.

Adolescence—Seeking Romantic Love

Iron John, by Robert Bly (1990), *Women Who Run with the Wolves*, by Clarissa Pinkola Estés (1993), and *Men and the Water of Life*, by Michael Meade (1992), show the life stages men and women go through, and their relationships in each life stage, as symbolized in folktales.

For more about developing awareness of hidden elements of your personality, read *Romancing the Shadow* edited by Connie Zweig and Steve Wolf (1996). The chapter about romantic partners shows how a projected ideal shatters, and how couples can pick up the pieces and use the experience to grow. Another chapter discusses how the negative qualities of each Greek god and goddess archetype sabotage relationships.

Three Black Skirts: All You Need To Survive, by Anna Johnson (1998) and *The Go-Girl Guide: Surviving Your 20s With Savvy, Soul, and Style*, by Julia Bourland (2000) are advice books for twenty-something women. *The Go-Girl Guide* has better relationship advice, but a 23-year-old told me that *Three Black Skirts* has better fashion advice. Both provide good advice about careers and finances.

QUOTATIONS AND MENTIONS

Evolution's End, by Joseph Chilton Pearce (1992), page 73.

The Picture of Dorian Gray, by Oscar Wilde (1890), page 76.

Coming Alive With Love, by Barbara De Angelis (1985), page 77.

The Go-Girl Guide, by Julia Bourland (2000), page 78.

How To Win Friends and Influence People, by Dale Carnegie (1936), page 81.

The Little Prince, by Antoine de Saint-Exupery (1943), page 83.

A Little More About Me, by Pam Houston (1999), page 84.

The Spirit of Intimacy, by Sobonfu Somé (2000), page 86.

What Our Mothers Didn't Teach Us, by Danielle Crittenden (1999), page 86.

Flirting

For more about flirting, see *Secrets of Sexual Body Language,* by Martin Lloyd-Elliott (1995). This book is beautiful, well-written, and well-produced. Every page has color photographs, of great-looking men and women. Twelve chapters cover everything from personal space zones to eye movements to how to kiss. The chapter on peek-a-boo is especially good.

QUOTATIONS AND MENTIONS

The Rules, by Ellen Fein and Sherrie Schneider (1995), page 97.

Coming Alive With Love, by Barbara De Angelis (1985), page 97.

How To Win Friends and Influence People, by Dale Carnegie (1936), pages 99–102.

The Language of Clothes, by Alison Lurie (2nd edition, 2000), page 107.

Big Hair: A Journey into the Transformation of Self, by Grant McCracken (1996), page 107.

House as a Mirror of Self: Exploring the Deeper Meaning of Home, by Clare Cooper Marcus and James Yandell (1995), page 108.

Personal Ads

QUOTATIONS AND MENTIONS

Paths to Marriage, by Bernard Murstein (1986), page 112.

Dating

QUOTATIONS AND MENTIONS

The Open Mind, by Dawna Markova (1991), page 122.

Seduction

QUOTATIONS AND MENTIONS

Our Bodies, Ourselves, by the Boston Women's Health Collective (1998), page 127.

The Social Impact of AIDS in the United States, by Albert Y. Jonsen and Jeff Stryker (1993), page 130.

Good Vibrations: The New Complete Guide to Vibrators, by Joani Blank (2000), page 130.

Sex in America: A Definitive Survey, by Robert T. Michael, John H. Gagnon, Edward O. Laumann, and Gina Bari Kolata (1994), page 134.

The Sweet Potato Queens' Book of Love, by Jill Conner Browne (1999), pages 136 and 137.

How To Please a Woman In and Out of Bed, by Daylle Deanna Schwartz (2001), page 137.

Shakespeare's Sonnets and Poems, edited by Louis B. Wright and Virginia A. Lamar (1988), page 137.

The Essential Rumi, translated by Coleman Barks (1997), page 137.

Becoming a Couple

For more about switching gender roles in dating, read *Getting To "I Do,"* by Patricia Allen and Sandra Harmon (1994). The authors believe that relation-  ships work when one partner uses masculine behavior and the other partner uses feminine behavior. A man and a woman may take either role, but a relationship breaks down when both individuals use masculine behavior (resulting in competition), or both use feminine behavior (needing, but not getting, emotional support).

A Fine Romance: The Passage of Courtship from Meeting to Marriage, by Judith Sills (1987), is the best book I've read about the transition from dating to committed relationships. The book also discusses the coded communication of flirtation, moving from dating to seduction, negotiation to work out problems, and commitment to marriage.

Why Do Fools Fall in Love: Experiencing the Magic, Mystery, and Meaning of Successful Relationships, edited by Janice R. Levine and Howard Markman (2000), is about the transition from loving your projected ideal to loving your real partner.

QUOTATIONS AND MENTIONS

The Rules, by Ellen Fein and Sherrie Schneider (1995), page 139.

Passionate Marriage, by David Schnarch (1997), page 142

Conflict in Relationships

How to Love a Woman: On Intimacy and the Erotic Life of Women, by Clarissa Pinkola Estés (1993), would be better titled "The Birth-Death-Rebirth Cycle of Intimate Relationships." Relationships start with high expectations. Sooner or later, scary, ugly, disturbing things happen. Expect this cycle. Staying emotionally committed through crises leads to a deeper relationship.

QUOTATIONS AND MENTIONS

Passionate Marriage, by David Schnarch (1997), page 150.

Reporting Live, by Lesley Stahl (2000), page 151.

The Emotional Revolution, by Norman Rosenthal (2002), page 152.

Emotional Control Systems

The emotional control systems are from *Affective Neuroscience: The Foundations of Human and Animal Emotions*, by Jaak Panksepp (1999).

    Goddesses in Everywoman (1984) and *Gods in Everyman* (1989), both by Jean Shinoda Bolen, present the Greek gods and goddesses as personality types. Each god or goddess has a 25- to 30-page chapter presenting mythology, the archetype in contemporary society, and the personality type from childhood through old age, including marriage and sex. Each chapter also identifies psychological difficulties associated with each archetype, and ways to grow to overcome these difficulties.

QUOTATIONS AND MENTIONS

Romancing the Shadow, by Connie Zweig and Steve Wolf (1997), page 155.

Poseidon–Athena

QUOTATIONS AND MENTIONS

Iron John, by Robert Bly (1990), page 162.

Apollo–Artemis

QUOTATIONS AND MENTIONS

Goddesses in Everywoman, by Jean Shinoda Bolen (1984), pages 173 and 174.

Hermes–Hestia

QUOTATIONS AND MENTIONS

Gods in Everyman, by Jean Shinoda Bolen (1989), page 181.

Dionysus–Demeter

For more about the relationship between the New Testament and older Dionysus myths, see *The Jesus Mysteries*, by Timothy Freke and Peter Gandy (1999).

For more about Osho, see *Golden Guru: The Strange Journey of Bhagwan Shree Rajneesh*, by James S. Gordon (1987).

Hades–Persephone

For more about Persephone behavior, including passivity and self-destructive behavior stages, see *The Wonder of Girls*, by Michael Gurian (2002). Gurian's *The Wonder of Boys* (1997) is also worth reading.

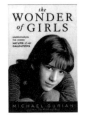

QUOTATIONS AND MENTIONS

Interview with the Vampire, by Anne Rice (1976), page 200.

Hamlet, by William Shakespeare (circa 1600), page 200.

The Glass Menagerie. by Tennessee Williams (1994), page 200.

I Never Promised You a Rose Garden, by Hannah Green (1988), page 200.

Screw the Roses, Send Me the Thorns: The Romance and Sexual Sorcery of Sadomasochism, by Philip Miller and Molly Devon (1995), page 203.

And, last but not least, *Sex News Daily* includes new studies about gender differences, social psychology, and relationship issues, as well as funny news stories involving sex. Subscribe to the free e-mail newsletter at http://www.sexnewsdaily.com/.

For more recommended books, please visit
http://www.FriendshipCenter.com/hearts/

AUTHOR BIOGRAPHY

Thomas David Kehoe has a bachelor's degree in philosophy from Reed College, an MBA from the University of Chicago, and currently studies transpersonal counseling psychology at Naropa University.

His father, Thomas F. Kehoe, is a retired Curator of Anthropology at the Milwaukee Public Museum. His mother, Alice B. Kehoe, is a retired Professor of Anthropology at Marquette University.

His hobbies include acting classes (which he's not good at) and running marathons (including 12th place at the 1999 RRCA National Marathon Championship in Napa, California).

REFERENCES

The paperback edition of this book doesn't include references. The references are in the hardcover edition and on
http://www.FriendshipCenter.com/hearts/

INDEX